What's Cooking

one pot

What's Cooking

one pot

A collection of must-have recipes for all occasions

This edition published in 2011

LOVE FOOD is an imprint of Parragon Books Ltd

Parragon

Queen Street House

4 Queen Street

Bath BA1 1HE, UK

ISBN: 978-1-4454-0317-5

Printed in China

Cover design by Talking Design

Cover image by Clive Streeter

Additional photography by Mike Cooper

Food styling by Sumi Glass and Lincoln Jefferson

Introduction by Christine McFadden

Notes for the Reader

This book uses both metric and imperial measurements. Follow the same units of measurement throughout; do not mix metric and imperial. All spoon measurements are level: teaspoons are assumed to be 5 ml, and tablespoons are assumed to be 15 ml. Unless otherwise stated, milk is assumed to be full fat, eggs and individual vegetables are medium, and pepper is freshly ground black pepper.

The times given are an approximate guide only. Preparation times differ according to the techniques used by different people and the cooking times may also vary from those given. Optional ingredients, variations or serving suggestions have not been included in the calculations.

Recipes using raw or very lightly cooked eggs should be avoided by infants, the elderly, pregnant women, convalescents and anyone suffering from an illness. Pregnant and breastfeeding women are advised to avoid eating peanuts and peanut products. Sufferers from nut allergies should be aware that some of the ready-made ingredients used in the recipes in this book may contain nuts. Always check the packaging before use.

CONTENTS

6 Introduction

10 Soups

40 Meat

70 Poultry

100 Fish & Seafood

130 Vegetables

160 Desserts

190 Index

INTRODUCTION

These days most of us lead action-packed lives, either at work or as a busy parent, or both. Time-consuming meal preparation, let alone clearing up afterwards, just doesn't fit in very easily. Yet most of us care about health and want to eat nutritious home-cooked food. What could be more satisfying than something simmering on the stove, filling the air with delicious aromas?

If you love cooking but are short of time, then *What's Cooking One Pot* will be a lifesaver. As the name suggests, all the dishes can be cooked in a single pot with other ingredients, leaving you with very little to wash up but plenty of time to get on with other things.

The one pot method is a relaxed and flexible way of cooking, easily adjusted to whatever ingredients you have in your fridge or store cupboard. If one ingredient is missing, it's usually possible to substitute another. If you're short of space or equipment, one pot cooking is ideal – you need just one pot and a single burner.

One pot cooking doesn't limit you to soups and stews, though the book contains plenty of recipes for these. In many parts of the world, cooking in a single pot is the norm, whether it's a cauldron, a wok, a tagine or a bean pot. Many dishes grew up out of necessity when food and fuel were scarce. Others were created for religious reasons – the Muslim Ramadan, for example, or the Jewish Sabbath when orthodox believers are forbidden to work or cook. The pot could be left to simmer slowly overnight, ready to serve at sunset the following day. In cold climates, it was the conviviality and friendship of communal eating that inspired many one pot dishes. Think of Swiss fondue, Hungarian goulash or Mongolian hot pot.

As the recipes in the book demonstrate, this no-frills way of cooking is the ultimate in convenience since everything is ready at the same time. It's the ideal food for solitary suppers or for feeding a crowd. Just put the pot on the table and tuck in.

GETTING STARTED

Although one pot cooking appears simple, it relies on a certain amount of pre-planning to ensure that things go smoothly. More importantly, getting organised from the start means you can relax and enjoy the actual process of cooking instead of running round the kitchen looking for missing utensils or, worse still, discovering too late that you've run out of a vital ingredient.

Before you start to cook:

- Read the recipe all the way through, then plan the sequence according to what needs soaking, chopping, precooking etc.
- Have the right tools and cookware to hand
- Make sure knives are sharp
- Wash fresh vegetables, fruits and herbs
- Assemble all the ingredients then measure or weigh them as necessary
- Complete any pre-preparation such as chopping or grating
- Have the prepared ingredients lined up in bowls, ready to add to the pot at the correct time
- Clear up as you go along

USEFUL UTENSILS

As well as basics such as knives and chopping boards, there are a number of additional utensils that make one pot cooking easier and safer.

Though you can happily leave the pot to simmer while you get on with something else, it's still important to keep track of temperature and time. Thermometers are essential for food safety, and a timer with a loud ring is invaluable for reminding you when the dish needs your attention. You'll also need spoons and spatulas for stirring, and tools for turning and lifting ingredients that are precooked in stages before they go into the pot. A sturdy long-handled fork or multi-pronged meat lifter are handy for large pieces of meat, while stainless steel spring-action tongs allow you to clasp smaller pieces of food securely. A perforated shallow skimmer is useful for removing froth and scum from the surface of stews.

Although one pot recipes are infinitely flexible, it's worth investing in proper measuring spoons and jugs, as well as

kitchen scales, especially if you are new to cooking. Once you gain experience and confidence, it's fine to add a pinch of this and a handful of that.

The joy of one pot meals is that they can be brought straight from oven to table. However, heat can damage unprotected surfaces, so it's a good idea to have a trivet or pot stand at the ready.

COOKWARE

For most of the recipes in this book, a few heavy-based saucepans and casseroles in varying sizes with tight-fitting lids make up the basic equipment. You'll also need a high-sided frying pan, a wok, good-quality roasting tins that won't warp or twist, and some shallow baking dishes for gratins and crumbles.

FRESH PRODUCE

Wholesome fresh vegetables, meat, poultry and fish add valuable nutrients to one pot meals, as well as colour, texture and appetizing flavours.

Vegetables

One of the most important source of vitamins, minerals and fibre, vegetables are packed with carotenoids (the plant form of vitamin A), vitamin C and vitamin E, which collectively protect against heart disease and some cancers.

Meat and poultry

Meat and poultry provide high quality protein, important minerals such as iron and zinc, and B vitamins, needed to release energy from food. Meat tends to be high in fat, so if you're trying to cut down, trim off any excess or choose lean cuts.

Fish and seafood

Dense-fleshed fish and seafood make marvellous one pot meals. They provide protein and essential minerals, while oily fish such as tuna are a unique source of omega-3 fatty acids that protect against heart disease and feed the brain.

Fresh herbs

A generous sprinkling of fresh herbs added at the end of cooking will provide delightful fragrance and colour to one pot meals.

STORE CUPBOARD ITEMS

A store cupboard judiciously stocked with a few essentials means you are never without the makings of a one pot meal.

Grains

Grains such as rice, barley, oats, quinoa and bulgar wheat contain a package of concentrated nutrients. Perked up with colourful spices and herbs, they form a nutritious base to which meat, fish and vegetables can be added as necessary.

Pulses

Dried pulses are packed with nutrients, and provide a mellow background to more strongly flavoured ingredients. Canned pulses are invaluable since you can add them to the pot without soaking or precooking.

Pasta

Short pasta shapes, from tiny star-shapes to coils and fat tubes, make the basis for endless one pot meals. Pasta shapes can be precooked or added to the pot with plenty of liquid.

Seeds and nuts

Crunchy seeds and nuts provide texture and, if chopped finely, can give body to the cooking liquid. Pumpkin, sunflower and sesame seeds are particularly nutritious, as are walnuts, almonds and Brazil nuts.

Sauces and pastes

A judicious splash of sauce or dollop of paste can perk up an otherwise bland dish. Soy sauce, Worcestershire sauce and Tabasco all have outstanding flavours, as do tomato purée, olive paste and mustards. Ready-made jars of ethnic sauces also add exciting flavours, and save time too.

Spices and dried herbs

For the best flavour, buy spices whole (including pepper), and grind them as needed. Rosemary, thyme and oregano are the best herbs to use dried; the more delicate varieties are better when fresh. Add spices and dried herbs at the early stages of cooking to bring out the full flavour.

SOUPS

CHUNKY VEGETABLE SOUP

Put the carrots, onion, garlic, potatoes, celery, mushrooms, tomatoes and stock into a large saucepan. Stir in the bay leaf and herbs. Bring to the boil, then reduce the heat, cover and simmer for 25 minutes.

Add the sweetcorn and cabbage and return to the boil. Reduce the heat, cover and simmer for 5 minutes, or until the vegetables are tender. Remove and discard the bay leaf. Season to taste with pepper.

Ladle into warmed bowls and serve at once with crusty bread rolls.

SERVES 6

2 carrots, sliced

1 onion, diced

1 garlic clove, crushed

350 g/12 oz new potatoes, diced

2 celery sticks, sliced

115 g/4 oz closed-cup mushrooms, quartered

400 g/14 oz canned chopped tomatoes in tomato juice

600 ml/1 pint vegetable stock

1 bay leaf

1 tsp dried mixed herbs or 1 tbsp chopped fresh mixed herbs

85 g/3 oz sweetcorn kernels, frozen or canned, drained

55 g/2 oz green cabbage, shredded

pepper

crusty wholemeal or white bread rolls, to serve

MINESTRONE

Heat the oil in a large saucepan. Add the garlic, onions and Parma ham and cook over a medium heat, stirring, for 3 minutes, until slightly softened. Add the red and orange peppers and the chopped tomatoes and cook for a further 2 minutes, stirring. Stir in the stock, then add the celery. Drain and add the borlotti beans along with the cabbage, peas and parsley. Season with salt and pepper. Bring to the boil, then lower the heat and simmer for 30 minutes.

Add the vermicelli to the pan. Cook for a further 10–12 minutes, or according to the instructions on the packet. Remove from the heat and ladle into serving bowls. Garnish with freshly grated Parmesan and serve with fresh crusty bread.

SERVES 4

2 tbsp olive oil

2 garlic cloves, chopped

2 red onions, chopped

75 g/2¾ oz Parma ham, sliced

1 red pepper, deseeded and chopped

1 orange pepper, deseeded and chopped

400 g/14 oz canned chopped tomatoes

1 litre/1¾ pints vegetable stock

1 celery stick, trimmed and sliced

400 g/14 oz canned borlotti beans

100 g/3½ oz green leafy cabbage, shredded

75 g/2¾ oz frozen peas, defrosted

1 tbsp chopped fresh parsley

75 g/2¾ oz dried vermicelli

salt and pepper

freshly grated Parmesan cheese, to garnish

fresh crusty bread, to serve

FRENCH
ONION SOUP

Thinly slice the onions. Heat the olive oil in a large, heavy-based saucepan, then add the onions and cook, stirring occasionally, for 10 minutes, until they are just beginning to brown. Stir in the chopped garlic, sugar and thyme, then reduce the heat and cook, stirring occasionally, for 30 minutes, or until the onions are golden brown.

Sprinkle in the flour and cook, stirring for 1–2 minutes. Stir in the wine. Gradually stir in the stock and bring to the boil, skimming off any scum that rises to the surface, then reduce the heat and simmer for 45 minutes. Meanwhile, preheat the grill to medium. Toast the bread on both sides under the grill. Rub the toast with the garlic clove.

Ladle the soup into 6 flameproof bowls set on a baking tray. Float a piece of toast in each bowl and divide the grated cheese among them. Place under the preheated grill for 2–3 minutes, or until the cheese has just melted. Garnish with thyme and serve.

SERVES 6

675 g/1 lb 8 oz onions

3 tbsp olive oil

4 garlic cloves, 3 chopped and
    1 peeled but kept whole

1 tsp sugar

2 tsp chopped fresh thyme

2 tbsp plain flour

125 ml/4 fl oz dry white wine

2 litres/3½ pints vegetable stock

6 slices of French bread

300 g/10½ oz Gruyère
    cheese, grated

fresh thyme sprigs, to garnish

BEEF GOULASH SOUP

Heat the oil in a large wide saucepan over a medium–high heat. Add the beef and sprinkle with salt and pepper. Fry until lightly browned.

Reduce the heat and add the onions and garlic. Cook for about 3 minutes, stirring frequently, until the onions are softened. Stir in the flour and continue cooking for 1 minute.

Add the water and stir to combine well, scraping the bottom of the pan to mix in the flour. Stir in the tomatoes, carrot, pepper, paprika, caraway seeds, oregano and stock.

Bring just to the boil. Reduce the heat, cover and simmer gently for about 40 minutes, stirring occasionally, until all the vegetables are tender.

Add the tagliatelle to the soup and simmer for a further 20 minutes, or until the tagliatelle is cooked.

Taste the soup and adjust the seasoning, if necessary. Ladle into warmed bowls and top each with a tablespoonful of soured cream. Garnish with coriander and serve.

SERVES 6

1 tbsp olive oil

500 g/1 lb 2 oz fresh lean beef mince

2 onions, finely chopped

2 garlic cloves, finely chopped

2 tbsp plain flour

225 ml/8 fl oz water

400 g/14 oz canned chopped tomatoes

1 carrot, finely chopped

225 g/8 oz red pepper, roasted, peeled, deseeded and chopped

1 tsp Hungarian paprika

¼ tsp caraway seeds

pinch of dried oregano

1 litre/1¾ pints beef stock

55 g/2 oz tagliatelle, broken into small pieces

salt and pepper

soured cream and sprigs of fresh coriander, to garnish

BACON & LENTIL SOUP

Heat a large, heavy-based saucepan or flameproof casserole. Add the bacon and cook over a medium heat, stirring, for 4–5 minutes, or until the fat runs. Add the chopped onion, carrots, celery, turnip and potato and cook, stirring frequently, for 5 minutes.

Add the lentils and bouquet garni and pour in the stock. Bring to the boil, reduce the heat and simmer for 1 hour, or until the lentils are tender.

Remove and discard the bouquet garni and season the soup to taste with pepper, and with salt, if necessary. Ladle into warmed soup bowls and serve immediately.

SERVES 4

450 g/1 lb thick, rindless smoked bacon rashers, diced

1 onion, chopped

2 carrots, sliced

2 celery sticks, chopped

1 turnip, chopped

1 large potato, chopped

85 g/3 oz Puy lentils

1 bouquet garni

1 litre/1¾ pints chicken stock

salt and pepper

ASIAN
LAMB SOUP

Trim all visible fat from the lamb and slice the meat thinly. Cut the slices into bite-sized pieces. Spread the meat in one layer on a plate and sprinkle over the garlic and 1 tablespoon of the soy sauce. Leave to marinate, covered, for at least 10 minutes or up to 1 hour.

Put the stock in a saucepan with the ginger, lemon grass, remaining soy sauce and the chilli purée. Bring just to the boil, reduce the heat, cover and simmer for 10–15 minutes.

When ready to serve the soup, drop the tomatoes, spring onions, beansprouts and fresh coriander leaves into the simmering stock.

Heat the oil in a frying pan and add the lamb with its marinade. Stir-fry the lamb just until it is no longer red and divide among warmed bowls.

Ladle over the hot stock and serve immediately.

SERVES 4

150 g/5½ oz lean tender lamb, such as neck fillet or leg steak

2 garlic cloves, very finely chopped

2 tbsp soy sauce

1.2 litres/2 pints chicken stock

1 tbsp grated fresh ginger

5-cm/2-inch piece lemon grass, sliced into very thin rounds

¼ tsp chilli purée, or to taste

6–8 cherry tomatoes, quartered

4 spring onions, finely sliced

50 g/1¾ oz beansprouts, snapped in half

2 tbsp fresh coriander leaves

1 tsp olive oil

CREAM OF CHICKEN SOUP

Melt the butter in a large saucepan over a medium heat. Add the shallots and cook, stirring, for 3 minutes, until slightly softened. Add the leek and cook for a further 5 minutes, stirring. Add the chicken, stock and herbs, and season with salt and pepper. Bring to the boil, then lower the heat and simmer for 25 minutes, until the chicken is tender and cooked through. Remove from the heat and leave to cool for 10 minutes.

Transfer the soup to a food processor or blender and process until smooth (you may need to do this in batches). Return the soup to the rinsed-out pan and warm over a low heat for 5 minutes.

Stir in the cream and cook for a further 2 minutes, then remove from the heat and ladle into serving bowls. Garnish with sprigs of thyme and serve immediately.

SERVES 4

3 tbsp butter

4 shallots, chopped

1 leek, sliced

450 g/1 lb skinless chicken breasts, chopped

600 ml/1 pint chicken stock

1 tbsp chopped fresh parsley

1 tbsp chopped fresh thyme, plus extra sprigs to garnish

175 ml/6 fl oz double cream

salt and pepper

COCK-A-LEEKIE SOUP

Heat the oil in a large saucepan over a medium heat, then add the onions, carrots and the 2 roughly chopped leeks. Sauté for 3–4 minutes until just golden brown.

Wipe the chicken inside and out and remove any excess skin and fat.

Place the chicken in the saucepan with the cooked vegetables and add the bay leaves. Pour in enough cold water to just cover and season well with salt and pepper. Bring to the boil, reduce the heat, then cover and simmer for 1–1½ hours. From time to time skim off any scum that forms.

Remove the chicken from the stock, remove and discard the skin, then remove all the meat. Cut the meat into neat pieces.

Strain the stock through a colander, discard the vegetables and bay leaves and return to the rinsed-out saucepan. Expect to have 1.2–1.4 litres/2–2½ pints of stock. If you have time, it is a good idea to allow the stock to cool so that the fat may be removed. If not, blot the fat off the surface with pieces of kitchen paper.

Heat the stock to simmering point, add the sliced leeks and prunes to the saucepan and heat for about 1 minute.

Return the chicken to the pan and heat through. Serve immediately in warmed deep dishes. Garnish with the parsley.

SERVES 6–8

2 tbsp olive oil

2 onions, roughly chopped

2 carrots, roughly chopped

5 leeks, 2 roughly chopped, 3 thinly sliced

1 chicken, weighing 1.3 kg/3 lb

2 bay leaves

6 prunes, sliced

salt and pepper

sprigs of fresh parsley, to garnish

THAI CHICKEN-COCONUT SOUP

Soak the dried noodles in a large bowl with enough lukewarm water to cover for 20 minutes, until soft. Alternatively, cook according to the packet instructions. Drain well and set aside.

Meanwhile, bring the stock to the boil in a large saucepan over a high heat. Lower the heat, add the lemon grass, ginger, lime leaves and chilli and simmer for 5 minutes. Add the chicken and continue simmering for a further 3 minutes, or until cooked. Stir in the coconut cream, nam pla and lime juice and continue simmering for 3 minutes. Add the beansprouts and spring onions and simmer for a further 1 minute. Taste and gradually add extra nam pla or lime juice at this point, if needed. Remove and discard the lemon grass stalk.

Divide the cellophane noodles between 4 bowls. Bring the soup back to the boil, then add the soup to each bowl. The heat of the soup will warm the noodles. To garnish, sprinkle with coriander leaves.

SERVES 4

115 g/4 oz dried cellophane noodles

1.2 litres/2 pints chicken or vegetable stock

1 lemon grass stalk, crushed

1-cm/½-inch piece fresh ginger, peeled and very finely chopped

2 fresh kaffir lime leaves, thinly sliced

1 fresh red chilli, or to taste, deseeded and thinly sliced

2 skinless, boneless chicken breasts, thinly sliced

200 ml/7 fl oz coconut cream

2 tbsp nam pla (Thai fish sauce)

1 tbsp fresh lime juice

55 g/2 oz beansprouts

4 spring onions, green part only, finely sliced

fresh coriander leaves, to garnish

TURKEY & LENTIL SOUP

Heat the oil in a large saucepan. Add the garlic and onion and cook over a medium heat, stirring, for 3 minutes, until slightly softened. Add the mushrooms, red pepper and tomatoes and cook for a further 5 minutes, stirring. Pour in the stock and red wine, then add the cauliflower, carrot and red lentils. Season to taste with salt and pepper. Bring to the boil, then lower the heat and simmer the soup gently for 25 minutes, until the vegetables are tender and cooked through.

Add the turkey and courgette to the pan and cook for 10 minutes. Stir in the shredded basil and cook for a further 5 minutes, then remove from the heat and ladle into serving bowls. Garnish with basil and serve immediately.

SERVES 4

1 tbsp olive oil

1 garlic clove, chopped

1 large onion, chopped

200 g/7 oz mushrooms, sliced

1 red pepper, deseeded and chopped

6 tomatoes, peeled, deseeded and chopped

1.2 litres/2 pints chicken stock

150 ml/5 fl oz red wine

85 g/3 oz cauliflower florets

1 carrot, chopped

200 g/7 oz red lentils

350 g/12 oz cooked turkey, chopped

1 courgette, chopped

1 tbsp shredded fresh basil

salt and pepper

sprigs of fresh basil, to garnish

DUCK WITH SPRING ONION SOUP

Slash the skin of the duck 3 or 4 times with a sharp knife and rub in the curry paste. Cook the duck breasts, skin-side down, in a wok or frying pan over a high heat for 2–3 minutes. Turn over, reduce the heat and cook for a further 3–4 minutes, until cooked through. Lift out and slice thickly. Set aside and keep warm.

Meanwhile, heat the oil in a wok or large frying pan and stir-fry half the spring onions, the garlic, ginger, carrots and red pepper for 2–3 minutes. Pour in the stock and add the chilli sauce, soy sauce and mushrooms. Bring to the boil, lower the heat and simmer for 4–5 minutes.

Ladle the soup into warmed bowls, top with the duck slices and garnish with the remaining spring onions. Serve immediately.

SERVES 2

2 duck breasts, skin on

2 tbsp red curry paste

2 tbsp vegetable or groundnut oil

bunch of spring onions, chopped

2 garlic cloves, crushed

5-cm/2-inch piece fresh ginger, grated

2 carrots, thinly sliced

1 red pepper, deseeded and cut into strips

1 litre/1¼ pints chicken stock

2 tbsp sweet chilli sauce

3–4 tbsp Thai soy sauce

400 g/14 oz canned straw mushrooms, drained

SEAFOOD CHOWDER

Discard any mussels with broken shells or any that refuse to close when tapped. Rinse and pull off any beards. Put the mussels in a large, heavy-based saucepan. Cover tightly and cook over a high heat for about 4 minutes, or until the mussels open, shaking the pan occasionally. Discard any that remain closed. When they are cool enough to handle, remove the mussels from their shells and set aside.

Put the flour in a mixing bowl and very slowly whisk in enough of the stock to make a thick paste. Whisk in a little more stock to make a smooth liquid.

Melt the butter in a heavy-based saucepan over a medium–low heat. Add the onion, cover and cook for 3 minutes, stirring frequently, until it softens.

Add the remaining fish stock and bring to the boil. Slowly whisk in the flour mixture until well combined and bring back to the boil, whisking constantly. Add the mussel cooking liquid. Season with salt, if needed, and pepper. Reduce the heat and simmer, partially covered, for 15 minutes.

Add the fish and mussels and continue simmering, stirring occasionally, for about 5 minutes, or until the fish is cooked and begins to flake.

Stir in the prawns and cream. Taste and adjust the seasoning. Simmer for a few minutes longer to heat through. Ladle into warmed bowls, sprinkle with dill and serve.

SERVES 6

1 kg/2 lb 4 oz live mussels

4 tbsp plain flour

1.5 litres/2¾ pints fish stock

1 tbsp butter

1 large onion, finely chopped

350 g/12 oz skinless white fish fillets, such as cod, sole or haddock

200 g/7 oz cooked or raw peeled prawns

300 ml/10 fl oz whipping cream or double cream

salt and pepper

snipped fresh dill, to garnish

BOUILLABAISSE

Heat the oil in a large pan over a medium heat. Add the garlic and onions and cook, stirring, for 3 minutes. Stir in the tomatoes, stock, wine, bay leaf, saffron and herbs. Bring to the boil, reduce the heat, cover and simmer for 30 minutes.

Meanwhile, soak the mussels in lightly salted water for 10 minutes. Scrub the shells under cold running water and pull off any beards. Discard any mussels with broken shells or any that refuse to close when tapped. Put the rest into a large pan with a little water, bring to the boil and cook over a high heat for 4 minutes. Remove from the heat and discard any that remain closed.

When the tomato mixture is cooked, rinse the fish fillets, pat dry and cut into chunks. Add to the pan and simmer for 5 minutes. Add the mussels, prawns and scallops and season with salt and pepper. Cook for 3 minutes, until the fish is cooked through. Remove from the heat, discard the bay leaf and ladle into serving bowls.

SERVES 4

100 ml/3½ fl oz olive oil

3 garlic cloves, chopped

2 onions, chopped

2 tomatoes, deseeded and chopped

700 ml/1¼ pints fish stock

400 ml/14 fl oz white wine

1 bay leaf

pinch of saffron threads

2 tbsp chopped fresh basil

2 tbsp chopped fresh parsley

200 g/7 oz live mussels

250 g/9 oz snapper or monkfish fillets

250 g/9 oz haddock fillets, skinned

200 g/7 oz prawns, peeled and deveined

100 g/3½ oz scallops

salt and pepper

SALMON & LEEK SOUP

Heat the oil in a heavy-based saucepan over a medium heat. Add the onion and leeks and cook for about 3 minutes until they begin to soften.

Add the potato, stock, water and bay leaf with a large pinch of salt. Bring to the boil, reduce the heat, cover and cook gently for about 25 minutes until the vegetables are tender. Remove the bay leaf.

Allow the soup to cool slightly, then transfer about half of it to a food processor or blender and process until smooth. (If using a food processor, strain off the cooking liquid and reserve. Purée half the soup solids with enough cooking liquid to moisten them, then combine with the remaining liquid.)

Return the puréed soup to the saucepan and stir to blend. Reheat gently over a medium–low heat.

Season the salmon with salt and pepper and add to the soup. Continue cooking for about 5 minutes, stirring occasionally, until the fish is tender and starts to break up. Stir in the cream, taste and adjust the seasoning, adding a little lemon juice, if using. Ladle into warmed bowls, garnish with chervil or parsley and serve.

SERVES 4

1 tbsp olive oil

1 large onion, finely chopped

3 large leeks, including green parts, thinly sliced

1 potato, finely diced

450 ml/16 fl oz fish stock

700 ml/1¼ pints water

1 bay leaf

300 g/10½ oz skinless salmon fillet, cut into 1-cm/½-inch cubes

80 ml/3 fl oz double cream

fresh lemon juice (optional)

salt and pepper

sprigs of fresh chervil or parsley, to garnish

MEAT

POT ROAST
WITH POTATOES
& DILL

Preheat the oven to 140°C/275°F/Gas Mark 1. Mix 2 tablespoons of the flour with the salt and pepper in a shallow dish. Dip the meat to coat. Heat the oil in a flameproof casserole and brown the meat all over. Transfer to a plate. Add half the butter to the casserole and cook the onion, celery, carrots, dill seed and thyme for 5 minutes. Return the meat and juices to the casserole.

Pour in the wine and enough stock to reach one third of the way up the meat. Bring to the boil, cover and cook in the oven for 3 hours, turning the meat every 30 minutes. After it has been cooking for 2 hours, add the potatoes and more stock if necessary.

When ready, transfer the meat and vegetables to a warmed serving dish. Strain the cooking liquid to remove any solids, then return the liquid to the casserole.

Mix the remaining butter and flour to a paste. Bring the cooking liquid to the boil. Whisk in small pieces of the flour and butter paste, whisking constantly until the sauce is smooth. Pour the sauce over the meat and vegetables. Sprinkle with the fresh dill to serve.

SERVES 6

2½ tbsp plain flour

1 tsp salt

¼ tsp pepper

1 rolled brisket joint, weighing 1.6 kg/3 lb 8 oz

2 tbsp vegetable oil

2 tbsp butter

1 onion, finely chopped

2 celery sticks, diced

2 carrots, peeled and diced

1 tsp dill seed

1 tsp dried thyme or oregano

350 ml/12 fl oz red wine

150–225 ml/5–8 fl oz beef stock

4–5 potatoes, cut into large chunks and boiled until just tender

2 tbsp chopped fresh dill, to serve

BEEF
STROGANOFF

Place the dried porcini in a bowl and cover with hot water. Leave to soak for 20 minutes. Meanwhile, cut the beef against the grain into 5-mm/¼-inch thick slices, then into 1-cm/½-inch long strips, and reserve.

Drain the porcini, reserving the soaking liquid, and chop. Strain the soaking liquid through a fine-mesh sieve or coffee filter and reserve.

Heat half the oil in a large frying pan. Add the shallots and cook over a low heat, stirring occasionally, for 5 minutes, or until softened. Add the soaked porcini, reserved soaking water and whole chestnut mushrooms and cook, stirring frequently, for 10 minutes, or until almost all of the liquid has evaporated, then transfer the mixture to a plate.

Heat the remaining oil in the frying pan, add the beef and cook, stirring frequently, for 4 minutes, or until browned all over. You may need to do this in batches. Return the mushroom mixture to the frying pan and season to taste with salt and pepper. Place the mustard and cream in a small bowl and stir to mix, then fold into the meat and mushroom mixture. Heat through gently, then serve with freshly cooked pasta, garnished with chives.

SERVES 4

15 g/½ oz dried porcini

350 g/12 oz beef fillet

2 tbsp olive oil

115 g/4 oz shallots, sliced

175 g/6 oz chestnut mushrooms

½ tsp Dijon mustard

5 tbsp double cream

salt and pepper

freshly cooked pasta, to serve

fresh chives, to garnish

CHILLI CON CARNE

Preheat the oven to 160ºC/325ºF/Gas Mark 3. Using a sharp knife, cut the beef into 2-cm/¾-inch cubes. Heat the vegetable oil in a large flameproof casserole dish and fry the beef over a medium heat until well sealed on all sides. Remove the beef from the casserole with a slotted spoon and reserve until required.

Add the onion and garlic to the casserole and fry until lightly browned; then stir in the flour and cook for 1–2 minutes.

Stir in the tomato juice and tomatoes and bring to the boil. Return the beef to the casserole and add the chilli sauce, cumin and salt and pepper to taste. Cover and cook in the preheated oven for 1½ hours, or until the beef is almost tender.

Stir in the kidney beans, oregano and parsley, and adjust the seasoning to taste, if necessary. Cover the casserole and return to the oven for 45 minutes. Serve on a bed of freshly cooked rice, garnished with sprigs of fresh herbs and accompanied by tortillas.

SERVES 4

750 g/1 lb 10 oz lean
  stewing steak

2 tbsp vegetable oil

1 large onion, sliced

2–4 garlic cloves, crushed

1 tbsp plain flour

425 ml/15 fl oz tomato juice

400 g/14 oz canned tomatoes

1–2 tbsp sweet chilli sauce

1 tsp ground cumin

425 g/15 oz canned red kidney
  beans, drained and rinsed

½ teaspoon dried oregano

1–2 tbsp chopped fresh parsley

salt and pepper

sprigs of fresh herbs, to garnish

freshly cooked rice and tortillas,
  to serve

PEPPER POT-STYLE STEW

Trim any fat or gristle from the beef and cut into 2.5-cm/1-inch chunks. Toss the beef in the flour until well coated and reserve any remaining flour.

Heat the oil in a large, heavy-based saucepan and cook the onion, garlic, chilli and celery with the cloves and allspice, stirring frequently, for 5 minutes, or until softened. Add the beef and cook over a high heat, stirring frequently, for 3 minutes, or until browned on all sides and sealed. Sprinkle in the reserved flour and cook, stirring constantly, for 2 minutes, then remove from the heat.

Add the hot pepper sauce and gradually stir in the stock, then return to the heat and bring to the boil, stirring. Reduce the heat, cover and simmer, stirring occasionally, for 1½ hours.

Add the squash and red pepper to the saucepan and simmer for a further 15 minutes. Add the tomatoes and okra and simmer for a further 15 minutes, or until the beef is tender. Serve with the wild rice.

SERVES 4

450 g/1 lb braising beef steak

1½ tbsp plain flour

2 tbsp olive oil

1 Spanish onion, chopped

3–4 garlic cloves, crushed

1 fresh green chilli, deseeded and chopped

3 celery sticks, sliced

4 whole cloves

1 tsp ground allspice

1–2 teaspoons hot pepper sauce, or to taste

600 ml/1 pint beef stock

225 g/8 oz deseeded and peeled squash, such as acorn, cut into small chunks

1 large red pepper, deseeded and chopped

4 tomatoes, roughly chopped

115 g/4 oz okra, trimmed and halved

freshly cooked wild rice, to serve

BEEF IN BEER WITH HERB DUMPLINGS

Preheat the oven to 160°C/325°F/Gas Mark 3. Heat the oil in a flameproof casserole. Add the onions and carrots and cook over a low heat, stirring occasionally, for 5 minutes, or until the onions are softened. Meanwhile, place the flour in a polythene bag and season with salt and pepper. Add the stewing steak to the bag, tie the top and shake well to coat. Do this in batches, if necessary.

Remove the vegetables from the casserole with a slotted spoon and reserve. Add the stewing steak to the casserole, in batches, and cook, stirring frequently, until browned all over. Return all the meat and the onions and carrots to the casserole and sprinkle in any remaining seasoned flour. Pour in the stout and add the sugar, bay leaves and thyme. Bring to the boil, cover and transfer to the preheated oven to bake for 1¾ hours.

To make the herb dumplings, sift the flour and salt into a bowl. Stir in the suet and parsley and add enough of the water to make a soft dough. Shape into small balls between the palms of your hands. Add to the casserole and return to the oven for 30 minutes. Remove and discard the bay leaves. Serve immediately, sprinkled with chopped parsley.

SERVES 6

2 tbsp sunflower oil

2 large onions, thinly sliced

8 carrots, sliced

4 tbsp plain flour

1.25 kg/2 lb 12 oz stewing steak, cut into cubes

425 ml/15 fl oz stout

2 tsp muscovado sugar

2 bay leaves

1 tbsp chopped fresh thyme

salt and pepper

herb dumplings

115 g/4 oz self-raising flour

pinch of salt

55 g/2 oz shredded suet

2 tbsp chopped fresh parsley, plus extra to garnish

about 4 tbsp water

PORK CHOPS WITH PEPPERS & SWEETCORN

Heat the oil in a large, flameproof casserole. Add the pork chops in batches and cook over a medium heat, turning occasionally, for 5 minutes, or until browned. Transfer the chops to a plate with a slotted spoon.

Add the chopped onion to the casserole and cook, stirring occasionally, for 5 minutes, or until softened. Add the garlic and peppers and cook, stirring occasionally for a further 5 minutes. Stir in the sweetcorn kernels with their juices and the parsley, and season to taste with salt and pepper.

Return the chops to the casserole, spooning the vegetable mixture over them. Cover and simmer for 30 minutes, or until tender. Serve immediately with mashed potatoes.

SERVES 4

1 tbsp sunflower oil

4 pork chops, trimmed of visible fat

1 onion, chopped

1 garlic clove, finely chopped

1 green pepper, deseeded and sliced

1 red pepper, deseeded and sliced

325 g/11½ oz canned sweetcorn kernels

1 tbsp chopped fresh parsley

salt and pepper

mashed potatoes, to serve

PAPRIKA PORK

Cut the pork into 4-cm/ 1½-inch cubes. Heat the oil and butter in a large saucepan. Add the pork and cook over a medium heat, stirring, for 5 minutes, or until browned. Transfer to a plate with a slotted spoon.

Add the chopped onion to the saucepan and cook, stirring occasionally, for 5 minutes, or until softened. Stir in the paprika and flour and cook, stirring constantly, for 2 minutes. Gradually stir in the stock and bring to the boil, stirring constantly.

Return the pork to the saucepan, add the sherry and sliced mushrooms and season to taste with salt and pepper. Cover and simmer gently for 20 minutes, or until the pork is tender. Stir in the soured cream and serve.

SERVES 4

675 g/1 lb 8 oz pork fillet

2 tbsp sunflower oil

25 g/1 oz butter

1 onion, chopped

1 tbsp paprika

25 g/1 oz plain flour

300 ml/10 fl oz chicken stock

4 tbsp dry sherry

115 g/4 oz mushrooms, sliced

salt and pepper

150 ml/5 fl oz soured cream

SAUSAGE & BEAN CASSEROLE

Prick the sausages all over with a fork. Heat 2 tablespoons of the oil in a large, heavy frying pan. Add the sausages and cook over a low heat, turning frequently, for 10–15 minutes, until evenly browned and cooked through. Remove them from the frying pan and keep warm. Drain off the oil and wipe out the pan with kitchen paper.

Heat the remaining oil in the frying pan. Add the onion, garlic and pepper to the frying pan and cook for 5 minutes, stirring occasionally, or until softened.

Add the tomatoes to the frying pan and leave the mixture to simmer for about 5 minutes, stirring occasionally, or until slightly reduced and thickened.

Stir the sun-dried tomato paste, cannellini beans and Italian sausages into the mixture in the frying pan. Cook for 4–5 minutes or until the mixture is piping hot. Add 4–5 tablespoons of water, if the mixture becomes too dry during cooking.

Transfer to serving plates and serve with mashed potatoes.

SERVES 4

8 Italian sausages

3 tbsp olive oil

1 large onion, chopped

2 garlic cloves, chopped

1 green pepper, deseeded and sliced

225 g/8 oz canned chopped tomatoes, skinned and chopped or 400 g/14 oz can tomatoes, chopped

2 tbsp sun-dried tomato paste

400 g/14 oz canned cannellini beans

mashed potatoes or rice, to serve

RED CURRY PORK WITH PEPPERS

Heat the oil in a wok or large frying pan and fry the onion and garlic for 1–2 minutes, until they are softened but not browned.

Add the pork slices and stir-fry for 2–3 minutes until browned all over. Add the pepper, mushrooms and curry paste.

Dissolve the coconut in the stock and add to the wok with the soy sauce. Bring to the boil and simmer for 4–5 minutes until the liquid has reduced and thickened.

Add the tomatoes and coriander and cook for 1–2 minutes before serving with noodles.

SERVES 4

2 tbsp vegetable or groundnut oil

1 onion, roughly chopped

2 garlic cloves, chopped

450 g/1 lb pork fillet, thickly sliced

1 red pepper, deseeded and cut into squares

175 g/6 oz mushrooms, quartered

2 tbsp Thai red curry paste

115 g/4 oz creamed coconut, chopped

300 ml/½ pint pork or vegetable stock

2 tbsp Thai soy sauce

4 tomatoes, peeled, deseeded and chopped

handful of fresh coriander, chopped

boiled noodles or rice, to serve

LAMB WITH PEARS

Preheat the oven to 160°C/325°F/Gas Mark 3. Heat the olive oil in a flameproof casserole over a medium heat. Add the lamb and cook, turning frequently, for 5–10 minutes, or until browned on all sides.

Arrange the pear quarters on top, then sprinkle over the ginger. Cover with the potatoes. Pour in the cider and season to taste with salt and pepper. Cover and cook in the preheated oven for 1¼ hours.

Trim the stalk ends of the green beans. Remove the casserole from the oven and add the beans, then re-cover and return to the oven for a further 30 minutes. Taste and adjust the seasoning. Sprinkle with the chives and serve.

SERVES 4

1 tbsp olive oil

1 kg/2 lb 4 oz best end-of-neck lamb cutlets, trimmed of visible fat

6 pears, peeled, cored and quartered

1 tsp ground ginger

4 potatoes, diced

4 tbsp dry cider

450 g/1 lb green beans

2 tbsp snipped fresh chives, to garnish

salt and pepper

CINNAMON LAMB CASSEROLE

Season the flour with salt and pepper to taste then put it with the lamb in a polythene bag, hold the top closed and shake until the lamb cubes are lightly coated all over. Remove the lamb from the bag, shake off any excess flour and set aside.

Heat the oil in a large, flameproof casserole and cook the onions and garlic, stirring frequently, for 5 minutes, or until softened. Add the lamb and cook over a high heat, stirring frequently, for 5 minutes, or until browned on all sides and sealed.

Stir the wine, vinegar and tomatoes and their juice into the casserole, scraping any sediment from the base of the casserole, and bring to the boil. Reduce the heat and add the raisins, cinnamon, sugar and bay leaf. Season to taste with salt and pepper. Cover and simmer gently for 2 hours, or until the lamb is tender.

Meanwhile, make the topping. Put the yogurt into a small serving bowl, stir in the garlic and season to taste with salt and pepper. Cover and chill in the refrigerator until required.

Discard the bay leaf and serve hot, topped with a spoonful of the garlicky yogurt and dusted with paprika.

SERVES 6

2 tbsp plain flour

1 kg/2 lb 4 oz lean boneless lamb, cubed

2 tbsp olive oil

2 large onions, sliced

1 garlic clove, finely chopped

300 ml/10 fl oz full-bodied red wine

2 tbsp red wine vinegar

400 g/14 oz canned chopped tomatoes

55 g/2 oz seedless raisins

1 tbsp ground cinnamon

pinch of sugar

1 bay leaf

salt and pepper

paprika, to garnish

topping

150 ml/5 fl oz natural Greek-style yogurt

2 garlic cloves, crushed

salt and pepper

LAMB STEW WITH CHICKPEAS

Preheat the oven to 160°C/325°F/Gas Mark 4. Heat 4 tablespoons of the oil in a large, heavy-based flameproof casserole over a medium–high heat. Reduce the heat, add the chorizo and fry for 1 minute. Transfer to a plate. Add the onions to the casserole and fry for 2 minutes, then add the garlic and continue frying for 3 minutes, or until the onions are soft, but not brown. Remove from the casserole and set aside.

Heat the remaining 2 tablespoons of oil in the casserole. Add the lamb cubes in a single layer without over-crowding the casserole, and fry until browned on each side; work in batches, if necessary.

Return the onion mixture and chorizo to the casserole with all the lamb. Stir in the stock, wine, vinegar, tomatoes with their juices and salt and pepper to taste. Bring to the boil, scraping any glazed bits from the base of the casserole. Reduce the heat and stir in the thyme, bay leaves and paprika.

Transfer to the preheated oven and cook, covered, for 40–45 minutes until the lamb is tender. Stir in the chickpeas and return to the oven, uncovered, for 10 minutes, or until they are heated through and the juices are reduced.

Taste and adjust the seasoning. Serve garnished with thyme.

SERVES 4–6

6 tbsp olive oil

225 g/8 oz chorizo sausage, cut into 5-mm/¼-inch thick slices, casings removed

2 large onions, chopped

6 large garlic cloves, crushed

900 g/2 lb boned leg of lamb, cut into 5-cm/2-inch chunks

250 ml/9 fl oz lamb stock or water

125 ml/4 fl oz red wine, such as Rioja or Tempranillo

2 tbsp sherry vinegar

800 g/1 lb 12 oz canned chopped tomatoes

4 sprigs fresh thyme, plus extra to garnish

2 bay leaves

½ tsp sweet Spanish paprika

800 g/1 lb 12 oz canned chickpeas, rinsed and drained

salt and pepper

IRISH STEW

Preheat the oven to 160°C/325°F/Gas Mark 3. Spread the flour on a plate and season with salt and pepper. Roll the pieces of lamb in the flour to coat, shaking off any excess, and arrange in the base of a casserole.

Layer the onions, carrots and potatoes on top of the lamb.

Sprinkle in the thyme and pour in the stock, then cover and cook in the preheated oven for 2½ hours. Garnish with the chopped fresh parsley and serve straight from the casserole.

SERVES 4

4 tbsp plain flour

1.3 kg/3 lb middle neck of lamb, trimmed of visible fat

3 large onions, chopped

3 carrots, sliced

450 g/1 lb potatoes, quartered

½ tsp dried thyme

850 ml/1½ pints hot beef stock

salt and pepper

2 tbsp chopped fresh parsley, to garnish

LAMB SHANKS

Dry-fry the coriander and cumin seeds until fragrant, then pound with the cinnamon, chilli and 2 garlic cloves in a mortar and pestle. Stir in half the oil and the lime rind. Rub the spice paste all over the lamb and marinate for 4 hours.

Preheat the oven to 200°C/400°F/Gas Mark 6. Heat the remaining oil in a flameproof casserole and cook the lamb, turning frequently, until evenly browned. Chop the remaining garlic and add to the casserole with the onions, carrots, celery and lime, then pour in enough stock or water to cover. Stir in the tomato purée, add the herbs and season with salt and pepper.

Cover and cook in the preheated oven for 30 minutes. Reduce the oven temperature to 160°C/325°F/Gas Mark 3 and cook for a further 3 hours, or until very tender.

Transfer the lamb to a dish. Strain the cooking liquid to remove any solids, then return the liquid to the casserole. Boil until reduced and thickened. Serve the lamb with the sauce poured over it, garnished with sprigs of rosemary.

SERVES 6

1 tsp coriander seeds

1 tsp cumin seeds

1 tsp ground cinnamon

1 fresh green chilli, deseeded and finely chopped

1 garlic bulb, separated into cloves

125 ml/4 fl oz groundnut or sunflower oil

grated rind of 1 lime

6 lamb shanks

2 onions, chopped

2 carrots, chopped

2 celery sticks, chopped

1 lime, chopped

about 700 ml/1¼ pints beef stock or water

1 tsp sun-dried tomato purée

2 fresh mint sprigs

2 fresh rosemary sprigs, plus extra to garnish

salt and pepper

POULTRY

ITALIAN-STYLE ROAST CHICKEN

Preheat the oven to 190°C/375°F/Gas Mark 5. Rinse the chicken inside and out with cold water and drain well. Carefully cut between the skin and the top of the breast meat using a small pointed knife. Slide a finger into the slit and carefully enlarge it to form a pocket. Continue until the skin is completely lifted away from both breasts and the tops of the legs.

Chop the leaves from 3 rosemary stems. Mix with the feta cheese, sun-dried tomato purée, butter, and pepper to taste, then spoon under the skin. Put the chicken in a large roasting tin, cover with foil and cook in the preheated oven, calculating the cooking time as 20 minutes per 500 g/1 lb 2 oz, plus 20 minutes.

Break the garlic bulb into cloves but do not peel. Add the vegetables and garlic to the roasting tin. After 40 minutes, drizzle with oil, tuck in a few stems of rosemary and season with salt and pepper. Cook for the remaining calculated time, removing the foil for the last 40 minutes to brown the chicken.

Transfer the chicken to a serving platter. Place some of the vegetables around the chicken and transfer the remainder to a warmed serving dish. Spoon the fat out of the roasting tin (it will be floating on top) and stir the flour into the remaining cooking juices. Place the roasting tin on top of the hob and cook over a medium heat for 2 minutes, then gradually stir in the stock. Bring to the boil, stirring until thickened and season to taste. Strain into a gravy boat and serve with the chicken.

SERVES 6

2.5 kg/5 lb 8 oz chicken

fresh rosemary sprigs

175 g/6 oz feta cheese, coarsely grated

2 tbsp sun-dried tomato purée

60 g/2 oz butter, softened

1 bulb garlic

1 kg/2 lb 4 oz new potatoes, halved if large

1 each red, green and yellow pepper, deseeded and cut into chunks

3 courgettes, thinly sliced

2 tbsp olive oil

2 tbsp plain flour

600 ml/1 pint chicken stock

salt and pepper

CHICKEN IN WHITE WINE

POULTRY

Preheat the oven to 160°C/325°F/Gas Mark 3. Melt half the butter with the oil in a flameproof casserole. Add the bacon and cook over a medium heat, stirring, for 5–10 minutes, or until golden brown. Transfer the bacon to a large plate. Add the onions and garlic to the casserole and cook over a low heat, stirring occasionally, for 10 minutes, or until golden. Transfer to the plate. Add the chicken and cook over a medium heat, stirring constantly, for 8–10 minutes, or until golden. Transfer to the plate.

Drain off any excess fat from the casserole. Stir in the wine and stock and bring to the boil, scraping any sediment off the base. Add the bouquet garni and season to taste. Return the bacon, onions and chicken to the casserole. Cover and cook in the preheated oven for 1 hour. Add the mushrooms, re-cover and cook for 15 minutes. Meanwhile, make a beurre manié by mashing the remaining butter with the flour in a small bowl.

Remove the casserole from the oven and set over a medium heat. Remove and discard the bouquet garni. Whisk in the beurre manié, a little at a time. Bring to the boil, stirring constantly, then serve, garnished with fresh herbs.

SERVES 4

55 g/2 oz butter

2 tbsp olive oil

2 rindless, thick streaky bacon rashers, chopped

115 g/4 oz baby onions, peeled

1 garlic clove, finely chopped

1.8 kg/4 lb chicken pieces

400 ml/14 fl oz dry white wine

300 ml/10 fl oz chicken stock

1 bouquet garni

115 g/4 oz button mushrooms

25 g/1 oz plain flour

salt and pepper

fresh mixed herbs, to garnish

COQ AU VIN

Melt half the butter with the olive oil in a large, flameproof casserole. Add the chicken and cook over a medium heat, stirring, for 8–10 minutes, or until golden brown all over. Add the bacon, onions, mushrooms and garlic.

Pour in the brandy and set it alight with a match or taper. When the flames have died down, add the wine, stock and bouquet garni and season to taste with salt and pepper. Bring to the boil, reduce the heat and simmer gently for 1 hour, or until the chicken pieces are cooked through and tender. Meanwhile, make a beurre manié by mashing the remaining butter with the flour in a small bowl.

Remove and discard the bouquet garni. Transfer the chicken to a large plate and keep warm. Stir the beurre manié into the casserole, a little at a time. Bring to the boil, return the chicken to the casserole and serve immediately, garnished with bay leaves.

SERVES 4

55 g/2 oz butter

2 tbsp olive oil

1.8 kg/4 lb chicken pieces

115 g/4 oz rindless smoked bacon, cut into strips

115 g/4 oz baby onions

115 g/4 oz chestnut mushrooms, halved

2 garlic cloves, finely chopped

2 tbsp brandy

225 ml/8 fl oz red wine

300 ml/10 fl oz chicken stock

1 bouquet garni

2 tbsp plain flour

salt and pepper

bay leaves, to garnish

HUNTER'S CHICKEN

Preheat the oven to 160°C/325°F/Gas Mark 3. Heat the butter and oil in a flameproof casserole and cook the chicken over a medium–high heat, turning frequently, for 10 minutes, or until golden all over and sealed. Using a slotted spoon, transfer to a plate.

Add the onions and garlic to the casserole and cook over a low heat, stirring occasionally, for 10 minutes, or until softened and golden. Add the tomatoes with their juice, the herbs, sun-dried tomato purée and wine, and season to taste with salt and pepper. Bring to the boil, then return the chicken portions to the casserole, pushing them down into the sauce.

Cover and cook in the preheated oven for 50 minutes. Add the mushrooms and cook for a further 10 minutes, or until the chicken is tender and the juices run clear when a skewer is inserted into the thickest part of the meat. Serve immediately.

SERVES 4

15 g/½ oz unsalted butter

2 tbsp olive oil

1.8 kg/4 lb skinned chicken portions

2 red onions, sliced

2 garlic cloves, finely chopped

400 g/14 oz canned chopped tomatoes

2 tbsp chopped fresh flat-leaf parsley

6 fresh basil leaves, torn

1 tbsp sun-dried tomato purée

150 ml/5 fl oz red wine

225 g/8 oz mushrooms, sliced

salt and pepper

CHICKEN RISOTTO WITH SAFFRON

Heat 55 g/2 oz of the butter in a deep saucepan. Add the chicken and onion and cook, stirring frequently, for 8 minutes, or until golden brown.

Add the rice and mix to coat in the butter. Cook, stirring constantly for 2–3 minutes, or until the grains are translucent. Add the wine and cook, stirring constantly, for 1 minute until reduced.

Mix the saffron with 4 tablespoons of the hot stock. Add to the rice and cook, stirring constantly, until it is absorbed.

Gradually add the remaining hot stock, a ladle at a time. Stir constantly and add more liquid as the rice absorbs each addition. Cook for 20 minutes, or until all the liquid is absorbed and the rice is creamy. Season to taste.

Remove the risotto from the heat and add the remaining butter. Mix well, then stir in the Parmesan until it melts. Spoon the risotto onto warmed plates and serve immediately.

SERVES 4

125 g/4½ oz butter

900 g/2 lb skinless, boneless chicken breasts, thinly sliced

1 large onion, chopped

500 g/1 lb 2 oz risotto rice

150 ml/5 fl oz white wine

1 tsp crumbled saffron threads

1.3 litres/2¼ pints simmering chicken stock

55 g/2 oz freshly grated Parmesan cheese

salt and pepper

PAPPARDELLE WITH CHICKEN & PORCINI

Place the porcini in a small bowl, add the hot water and leave to soak for 20 minutes. Meanwhile, place the tomatoes and their can juices in a heavy-based saucepan and break them up with a wooden spoon, then stir in the chilli. Bring to the boil, reduce the heat and simmer, stirring occasionally, for 30 minutes, or until reduced.

Remove the mushrooms from their soaking liquid with a slotted spoon, reserving the liquid. Sieve the liquid through a coffee filter paper or muslin-lined sieve into the tomatoes and simmer for a further 15 minutes.

Meanwhile, heat 2 tablespoons of the olive oil in a heavy-based frying pan. Add the chicken and cook, stirring frequently, until golden brown all over and tender. Stir in the mushrooms and garlic and cook for a further 5 minutes.

While the chicken is cooking, bring a large, heavy-based saucepan of lightly salted water to the boil. Add the pasta, return to the boil and cook for 8–10 minutes, or until tender but still firm to the bite. Drain well, transfer to a warmed serving dish, drizzle with the remaining olive oil and toss lightly. Stir the chicken mixture into the tomato sauce, season to taste with salt and pepper and spoon on top of the pasta. Toss lightly, sprinkle with parsley and serve immediately.

SERVES 4

40 g/1½ oz dried porcini mushrooms

175 ml/6 fl oz hot water

800 g/1 lb 12 oz canned chopped tomatoes

1 fresh red chilli, deseeded and finely chopped

3 tbsp olive oil

350 g/12 oz skinless, boneless chicken, cut into thin strips

2 garlic cloves, finely chopped

350 g/12 oz dried pappardelle

salt and pepper

2 tbsp chopped fresh flat-leaf parsley, to garnish

LOUISIANA CHICKEN

Heat the oil in a large, heavy-based saucepan or flameproof casserole. Add the chicken and cook over a medium heat, stirring, for 5–10 minutes, or until golden. Transfer the chicken to a plate with a slotted spoon.

Stir the flour into the oil and cook over a very low heat, stirring constantly, for 15 minutes, or until light golden. Do not let it burn. Add the onion, celery and green pepper and cook, stirring constantly, for 2 minutes. Add the garlic, thyme and chillies and cook, stirring, for 1 minute.

Stir in the tomatoes and their juices, then gradually stir in the stock. Return the chicken pieces to the saucepan, cover and simmer for 45 minutes, or until the chicken is cooked through and tender. Season to taste with salt and pepper, transfer to warmed serving plates and serve immediately, garnished with some lettuce leaves and a sprinkling of chopped thyme.

SERVES 4

5 tbsp sunflower oil

4 chicken portions

55 g/2 oz plain flour

1 onion, chopped

2 celery sticks, sliced

1 green pepper, deseeded and chopped

2 garlic cloves, finely chopped

2 tsp chopped fresh thyme

2 fresh red chillies, deseeded and finely chopped

400 g/14 oz canned chopped tomatoes

300 ml/10 fl oz chicken stock

salt and pepper

lamb's lettuce and chopped fresh thyme, to garnish

CHICKEN TAGINE

Heat the oil in a large saucepan over a medium heat, add the onion and garlic and cook for 3 minutes, stirring frequently. Add the chicken and cook, stirring constantly, for a further 5 minutes, or until sealed on all sides. Add the cumin and cinnamon sticks to the saucepan halfway through sealing the chicken.

Sprinkle in the flour and cook, stirring constantly, for 2 minutes. Add the aubergine, red pepper and mushrooms and cook for a further 2 minutes, stirring constantly.

Blend the tomato purée with the stock, stir into the saucepan and bring to the boil. Reduce the heat and add the chickpeas and apricots. Cover and simmer for 15–20 minutes, or until the chicken is tender.

Season with salt and pepper to taste and serve immediately, sprinkled with coriander.

SERVES 4

1 tbsp olive oil

1 onion, cut into small wedges

2–4 garlic cloves, sliced

450 g/1 lb skinless, boneless chicken breast, diced

1 tsp ground cumin

2 cinnamon sticks, lightly bruised

1 tbsp plain wholemeal flour

225 g/8 oz aubergine, diced

1 red pepper, deseeded and chopped

85 g/3 oz button mushrooms, sliced

1 tbsp tomato purée

600 ml/1 pint chicken stock

280 g/10 oz canned chickpeas, drained and rinsed

55 g/2 oz ready-to-eat dried apricots, chopped

salt and pepper

1 tbsp chopped fresh coriander, to garnish

BALTI CHICKEN

Heat the ghee in a large, heavy-based frying pan. Add the onions and cook over a low heat, stirring occasionally, for 10 minutes, or until golden. Add the sliced tomatoes, kalonji seeds, peppercorns, cardamom pods, cinnamon stick, chilli powder, garam masala, garlic purée and ginger purée, and season with salt to taste. Cook, stirring constantly, for 5 minutes.

Add the chicken and cook, stirring constantly, for 5 minutes, or until well coated in the spice paste. Stir in the yogurt. Cover and simmer, stirring occasionally, for 10 minutes.

Stir in the chopped coriander, chillies and lime juice. Transfer to a warmed serving dish, sprinkle with more chopped coriander and serve immediately.

SERVES 6

3 tbsp ghee or vegetable oil

2 large onions, sliced

3 tomatoes, sliced

½ tsp kalonji seeds

4 black peppercorns

2 cardamom pods

1 cinnamon stick

1 tsp chilli powder

1 tsp garam masala

1 tsp garlic purée

1 tsp ginger purée

700 g/1 lb 9 oz skinless, boneless chicken breasts or thighs, diced

2 tbsp natural yogurt

2 tbsp chopped fresh coriander, plus extra to garnish

2 fresh green chillies, deseeded and finely chopped

2 tbsp lime juice

salt

THAI GREEN CHICKEN CURRY

Heat 2 tablespoons of oil in a preheated wok or large, heavy-based frying pan. Add 2 tablespoons of the curry paste and stir-fry briefly until all the aromas are released.

Add the chicken, lime leaves and lemon grass and stir-fry for 3–4 minutes, until the meat is beginning to colour. Add the coconut milk and aubergines and simmer gently for 8–10 minutes, or until tender.

Stir in the fish sauce and serve immediately, garnished with Thai basil sprigs and lime leaves.

SERVES 4

2 tbsp groundnut or sunflower oil

2 tbsp ready-made Thai green curry paste

500 g/1 lb 2 oz skinless boneless chicken breasts, cut into cubes

2 kaffir lime leaves, roughly torn

1 lemon grass stalk, finely chopped

225 ml/8 fl oz canned coconut milk

16 baby aubergines, halved

2 tbsp Thai fish sauce

fresh Thai basil sprigs and kaffir lime leaves, thinly sliced, to garnish

ITALIAN TURKEY
CUTLETS

Preheat the grill to medium. Heat the oil in a flameproof casserole
or heavy-based frying pan. Add the turkey escalopes and cook
over a medium heat for 5–10 minutes, turning occasionally, until
golden. Transfer to a plate.

Add the red pepper and onion to the frying pan and cook over
a low heat, stirring occasionally, for 5 minutes, or until softened.
Add the garlic and cook for a further 2 minutes.

Return the turkey to the frying pan and add the passata,
wine and marjoram. Season to taste with salt and pepper. Bring
to the boil, then reduce the heat, cover and simmer, stirring
occasionally, for 25–30 minutes, or until the turkey is cooked
through and tender.

Stir in the cannellini beans and simmer for a further 5 minutes.
Sprinkle the breadcrumbs over the top and place under the
preheated grill for 2–3 minutes, or until golden. Serve, garnished
with fresh basil sprigs.

SERVES 4

1 tbsp olive oil

4 turkey escalopes or steaks

2 red peppers, deseeded
    and sliced

1 red onion, sliced

2 garlic cloves, finely chopped

300 ml/10 fl oz passata

150 ml/5 fl oz medium white wine

1 tbsp chopped fresh marjoram

400 g/14 oz canned cannellini
    beans, drained and rinsed

3 tbsp fresh white breadcrumbs

salt and pepper

fresh basil sprigs, to garnish

MEXICAN TURKEY

Preheat the oven to 160°C/325°F/Gas Mark 3. Spread the flour on a plate and season with salt and pepper. Coat the turkey fillets in the seasoned flour, shaking off any excess. Reserve any remaining seasoned flour.

Heat the oil in a flameproof casserole. Add the turkey fillets and cook over a medium heat, turning occasionally, for 5–10 minutes, or until golden. Transfer to a plate with a slotted spoon.

Add the onion and red pepper to the casserole. Cook over a low heat, stirring occasionally, for 5 minutes, or until softened. Sprinkle in the remaining seasoned flour and cook, stirring constantly, for 1 minute. Gradually stir in the stock, then add the raisins, chopped tomatoes, chilli powder, cinnamon, cumin and chocolate. Season to taste with salt and pepper. Bring to the boil, stirring constantly.

Return the turkey to the casserole, cover and cook in the preheated oven for 50 minutes. Serve immediately, garnished with sprigs of coriander.

SERVES 4

55 g/2 oz plain flour

4 turkey breast fillets

3 tbsp corn oil

1 onion, thinly sliced

1 red pepper, deseeded and sliced

300 ml/10 fl oz chicken stock

25 g/1 oz raisins

4 tomatoes, peeled, deseeded and chopped

1 tsp chilli powder

½ tsp ground cinnamon

pinch of ground cumin

25 g/1 oz plain chocolate, finely chopped or grated

salt and pepper

sprigs of fresh coriander, to garnish

DUCK LEGS
WITH OLIVES

Put the duck legs in the bottom of a flameproof casserole or a large, heavy-based frying pan with a tight-fitting lid. Add the tomatoes, garlic, onion, carrot, celery, thyme and olives and stir together. Season to taste with salt and pepper.

Turn the heat to high and cook, uncovered, until the ingredients begin to bubble. Reduce the heat to low, cover tightly and simmer for 1¼–1½ hours until the duck is very tender. Check occasionally and add a little water if the mixture appears to be drying out.

When the duck is tender, transfer it to a serving platter, cover and keep hot in a preheated warm oven. Leave the casserole uncovered, increase the heat to medium and cook, stirring, for about 10 minutes until the mixture forms a sauce. Stir in the orange rind, then taste and adjust the seasoning if necessary.

Mash the tender garlic cloves with a fork and spread over the duck legs. Spoon the sauce over the top. Serve at once.

SERVES 4

4 duck legs, all visible fat
    trimmed off

800 g/1 lb 12 oz canned tomatoes,
    chopped

8 garlic cloves, peeled but
    left whole

1 large onion, chopped

1 carrot, finely chopped

1 celery stick, finely chopped

3 sprigs fresh thyme

100 g/3½ oz Spanish green olives
    in brine, stuffed with pimientos,
    garlic or almonds, drained
    and rinsed

1 tsp finely grated orange rind

salt and pepper

DUCK JAMBALAYA-STYLE STEW

Remove and discard the skin and any fat from the duck breasts. Cut the flesh into bite-sized pieces.

Heat half the oil in a large deep frying pan and cook the duck, gammon and chorizo over a high heat, stirring frequently, for 5 minutes, or until browned on all sides and sealed. Using a slotted spoon, remove from the frying pan and set aside.

Add the onion, garlic, celery and chillies to the frying pan and cook over a medium heat, stirring frequently, for 5 minutes, or until softened. Add the green pepper, then stir in the stock, oregano, tomatoes and hot pepper sauce.

Bring to the boil, then reduce the heat and return the duck, gammon and chorizo to the frying pan. Cover and simmer, stirring occasionally, for 20 minutes, or until the duck and gammon are tender.

Serve immediately, garnished with parsley and accompanied by a green salad and rice.

SERVES 4

4 duck breasts, about 150 g/5½ oz each

2 tbsp olive oil

225 g/8 oz piece gammon, cut into small chunks

225 g/8 oz chorizo, outer casing removed

1 onion, chopped

3 garlic cloves, chopped

3 celery sticks, chopped

1–2 fresh red chillies, deseeded and chopped

1 green pepper, deseeded and chopped

600 ml/1 pint chicken stock

1 tbsp chopped fresh oregano

400 g/14 oz canned chopped tomatoes

1–2 tsp hot pepper sauce, or to taste

chopped fresh flat-leaf parsley, to garnish

green salad and freshly cooked rice, to serve

FISH & SEAFOOD

MONKFISH PARCELS

Preheat the oven to 190°C/375°F/Gas Mark 5. Cut 4 large pieces of foil, each about 23 cm/9 inches square. Brush them lightly with a little of the oil, then divide the courgettes and pepper among them.

Rinse the fish fillets under cold running water and pat dry with kitchen paper. Cut them in half, then put 1 piece on top of each pile of courgettes and pepper. Cut the bacon rashers in half and lay 3 pieces across each piece of fish. Season to taste with salt and pepper, drizzle over the remaining oil and close up the parcels. Seal tightly, transfer to an ovenproof dish and bake in the preheated oven for 25 minutes.

Remove from the oven, open each foil parcel slightly and serve with pasta and slices of olive bread.

SERVES 4

4 tsp olive oil

2 courgettes, sliced

1 large red pepper, peeled, deseeded and cut into strips

2 monkfish fillets, about 125 g/ 4½ oz each, skin and membrane removed

6 smoked streaky bacon rashers

salt and pepper

freshly cooked pasta and slices of olive bread, to serve

ROASTED MONKFISH

Preheat the oven to 200°C/400°F/Gas Mark 6. Remove the central bone from the fish if not already removed and make small slits down each fillet. Cut 2 of the garlic cloves into thin slivers and insert into the fish. Place the fish on a sheet of greaseproof paper, season to taste with salt and pepper and drizzle over 1 tablespoon of the oil. Bring the top edges together. Form into a pleat and fold over, then fold the ends underneath, completely encasing the fish. Reserve.

Put the remaining garlic cloves and all the vegetables into a roasting tin and drizzle with the remaining oil, turning the vegetables so that they are well coated in the oil.

Roast in the preheated oven for 20 minutes, turning occasionally. Put the fish parcel on top of the vegetables and cook for a further 15–20 minutes, or until the vegetables are tender and the fish is cooked.

Remove from the oven and open up the parcel. Cut the monkfish into thick slices. Arrange the vegetables on warmed serving plates, top with the fish slices and sprinkle with the basil. Serve immediately.

SERVES 4

675 g/1 lb 8 oz monkfish tail, skinned

4–5 large garlic cloves, peeled

3 tbsp olive oil

1 onion, cut into wedges

1 small aubergine, about 300 g/ 10½ oz, cut into chunks

1 red pepper, deseeded, cut into wedges

1 yellow pepper, deseeded, cut into wedges

1 large courgette, about 225 g/ 8 oz, cut into wedges

salt and pepper

1 tbsp shredded fresh basil, to garnish

MEDITERRANEAN SWORDFISH

Heat the oil in a large, heavy-based frying pan. Add the onion and celery and cook over a low heat, stirring occasionally, for 5 minutes, or until softened.

Meanwhile, roughly chop half the olives. Stir the chopped and whole olives into the saucepan with the tomatoes and capers and season to taste with salt and pepper.

Bring to the boil, then reduce the heat, cover and simmer gently, stirring occasionally, for 15 minutes.

Add the swordfish steaks to the frying pan and return to the boil. Cover and simmer, turning the fish once, for 20 minutes, or until the fish is cooked and the flesh flakes easily. Transfer the fish to serving plates and spoon the sauce over them. Garnish with fresh parsley sprigs and serve immediately.

SERVES 4

2 tbsp olive oil

1 onion, finely chopped

1 celery stick, finely chopped

115 g/4 oz green olives, stoned

450 g/1 lb tomatoes, chopped

3 tbsp bottled capers, drained

4 swordfish steaks, about
    140 g/5 oz each

salt and pepper

fresh flat-leaf parsley sprigs,
    to garnish

SICILIAN TUNA

Whisk all the marinade ingredients together in a small bowl. Put the tuna steaks in a large, shallow dish and spoon over 4 tablespoons of the marinade, turning until well coated. Cover and leave to marinate in the refrigerator for 30 minutes. Reserve the remaining marinade.

Heat a ridged pan over a high heat. Put the fennel and onions in a separate bowl, add the oil and toss well to coat. Add to the pan and cook for 5 minutes on each side until just beginning to colour. Transfer to 4 warmed serving plates, drizzle with the reserved marinade and keep warm.

Add the tuna steaks to the pan and cook, turning once, for 4–5 minutes until firm to the touch but still moist inside. Transfer the tuna to the serving plates and serve immediately with crusty rolls.

SERVES 4

4 tuna steaks, about 140 g/5 oz each

2 fennel bulbs, thickly sliced lengthways

2 red onions, sliced

2 tbsp extra virgin olive oil

crusty rolls, to serve

marinade

125 ml/4 fl oz extra virgin olive oil

4 garlic cloves, finely chopped

4 fresh red chillies, deseeded and finely chopped

juice and finely grated rind of 2 lemons

4 tbsp finely chopped fresh flat-leaf parsley

salt and pepper

CATALAN FISH STEW

Put the saffron threads in a heatproof jug with the water and leave for at least 10 minutes to infuse.

Heat the oil in a large, heavy-based flameproof casserole over a medium–high heat. Reduce the heat to low and cook the onion, stirring occasionally, for 10 minutes, or until golden but not browned. Stir in the garlic, thyme, bay leaves and red peppers and cook, stirring frequently, for 5 minutes, or until the peppers are softened and the onions have softened further.

Add the tomatoes and paprika and simmer, stirring frequently, for a further 5 minutes.

Stir in the stock, the saffron and its soaking liquid and the almonds and bring to the boil, stirring. Reduce the heat and simmer for 5–10 minutes, until the sauce reduces and thickens. Season to taste with salt and pepper.

Meanwhile, clean the mussels and clams by scrubbing or scraping the shells and pulling out any beards that are attached to the mussels. Discard any with broken shells or any that refuse to close when tapped.

Gently stir the hake into the stew so that it doesn't break up, then add the prawns, mussels and clams. Reduce the heat to very low, cover and simmer for 5 minutes, or until the hake is opaque, the mussels and clams have opened and the prawns have turned pink. Discard any mussels or clams that remain closed. Serve immediately.

SERVES 4–6

large pinch of saffron threads

4 tbsp almost-boiling water

6 tbsp olive oil

1 large onion, chopped

2 garlic cloves, finely chopped

1½ tbsp chopped fresh thyme leaves

2 bay leaves

2 red peppers, deseeded and roughly chopped

800 g/1 lb 12 oz canned chopped tomatoes

1 tsp smoked paprika

250 ml/9 fl oz fish stock

140 g/5 oz blanched almonds, toasted and finely ground

12–16 live mussels

12–16 live clams

600 g/1 lb 5 oz thick boned hake or cod fillets, skinned and cut into 5-cm/2-inch chunks

12–16 raw prawns, peeled and deveined

salt and pepper

PRAWN LAKSA

Peel and devein the prawns. Put the fish stock, salt and the prawn heads, shell and tails in a saucepan over a high heat and slowly bring to the boil. Lower the heat and simmer for 10 minutes.

Meanwhile, make the laksa paste. Put all the ingredients except the oil in a food processor and blend. With the motor running, slowly add up to 2 tablespoons of oil just until a paste forms. (If your food processor is too large to work efficiently with this small quantity, use a pestle and mortar, or make double the quantity and keep the leftovers tightly covered in the refrigerator to use another time.)

Heat the oil in a large saucepan over a high heat. Add the paste and stir-fry until it is fragrant. Strain the stock through a sieve lined with muslin. Stir the stock into the laksa paste, along with the coconut milk, nam pla and lime juice. Bring to the boil, then lower the heat, cover and simmer for 30 minutes.

Meanwhile, soak the noodles in a large bowl with enough lukewarm water to cover for 20 minutes, until soft. Alternatively, cook according to the packet instructions. Drain and set aside.

Add the prawns and beansprouts to the stew and continue simmering just until the prawns turn opaque and curl. Divide the noodles between 4 bowls and ladle the stew over, making sure everyone gets an equal share of the prawns. Garnish with the coriander and serve.

SERVES 4

20–24 large raw unpeeled prawns

450 ml/16 fl oz fish stock

pinch of salt

1 tsp groundnut oil

450 ml/16 fl oz coconut milk

2 tsp nam pla (Thai fish sauce)

½ tbsp lime juice

115 g/4 oz dried medium
   rice noodles

55 g/2 oz beansprouts

sprigs of fresh coriander,
   to garnish

laksa paste

6 coriander stalks with leaves

3 large garlic cloves, crushed

1 fresh red chilli, deseeded and
   chopped

1 lemon grass stalk, centre part
   only, chopped

2.5-cm/1-inch piece fresh ginger,
   peeled and chopped

1½ tbsp shrimp paste

½ tsp turmeric

2 tbsp groundnut oil

PRAWNS WITH COCONUT RICE

Place the mushrooms in a small bowl, cover with hot water and set aside to soak for 30 minutes. Drain, then cut off and discard the stalks and slice the caps.

Heat the oil in a wok and stir-fry the spring onions, coconut and chilli for 2–3 minutes, until lightly browned. Add the mushrooms and stir-fry for 3–4 minutes.

Add the rice and stir-fry for 2–3 minutes, then add the stock and bring to the boil. Lower the heat and add the coconut milk. Simmer for 10–15 minutes, until the rice is tender. Stir in the prawns and basil, heat through and serve.

SERVES 4

115 g/4 oz dried Chinese
 mushrooms

1 tbsp vegetable or groundnut oil

6 spring onions, chopped

55 g/2 oz desiccated coconut

1 fresh green chilli, deseeded
 and chopped

225 g/8 oz jasmine rice

150 ml/¼ pint fish stock

400 ml/14 fl oz coconut milk

350 g/12 oz cooked peeled prawns

6 sprigs fresh Thai basil

PRAWN & CHICKEN PAELLA

Soak the mussels in lightly salted water for 10 minutes. Put the saffron threads and water in a small bowl or cup and leave to infuse for a few minutes. Meanwhile, put the rice in a sieve and rinse in cold water until the water runs clear. Set aside.

Heat 3 tablespoons of the oil in a 30-cm/12-inch paella pan or ovenproof casserole. Cook the chicken thighs over a medium–high heat, turning frequently, for 5 minutes, or until golden and crispy. Using a slotted spoon, transfer to a bowl. Add the chorizo to the pan and cook, stirring, for 1 minute, or until beginning to crisp. Add to the chicken.

Heat the remaining oil in the pan and cook the onions, stirring frequently, for 2 minutes, then add the garlic and paprika and cook for a further 3 minutes, or until the onions are soft but not browned.

Add the drained rice, beans and peas and stir until coated in oil. Return the chicken and chorizo and any accumulated juices to the pan. Stir in the stock, saffron and its soaking liquid, and salt and pepper to taste and bring to the boil, stirring constantly. Reduce the heat to low and simmer, uncovered and without stirring, for 15 minutes, or until the rice is almost tender.

Arrange the mussels, prawns and red peppers on top, then cover and simmer, without stirring, for a further 5 minutes, or until the prawns turn pink and the mussels open. Discard any mussels that remain closed. Taste and adjust the seasoning if necessary. Sprinkle with the parsley and serve immediately.

SERVES 6–8

16 live mussels

½ tsp saffron threads

2 tbsp hot water

350 g/12 oz cups paella rice

6 tbsp olive oil

6–8 boned chicken thighs

140 g/5 oz Spanish chorizo sausage, sliced

2 large onions, chopped

4 large garlic cloves, crushed

1 tsp mild or hot Spanish paprika

100 g/3½ oz green beans, chopped

125 g/4½ oz frozen peas

1.3 litres/2¼ pints fish stock

16 raw prawns, peeled and deveined

2 red peppers, halved and deseeded, then grilled, peeled and sliced

salt and pepper

35 g/1¼ oz fresh chopped parsley, to garnish

MOULES MARINIÈRES

Clean the mussels by scrubbing or scraping the shells and pulling off any beards. Discard any with broken shells or any that refuse to close when tapped with a knife. Rinse the mussels under cold running water.

Pour the wine into a large, heavy-based saucepan, add the shallots and bouquet garni and season to taste with pepper. Bring to the boil over a medium heat. Add the mussels, cover tightly and cook, shaking the saucepan occasionally, for 5 minutes. Remove and discard the bouquet garni and any mussels that remain closed. Divide the mussels between 4 serving bowls with a slotted spoon. Tilt the pan to let any sand settle, then spoon the cooking liquid over the mussels, garnish with a bay leaf, and serve immediately with bread.

SERVES 4

2 kg/4 lb 8 oz live mussels

300 ml/10 fl oz dry white wine

6 shallots, finely chopped

1 bouquet garni

pepper

4 bay leaves, to garnish

crusty bread, to serve

SQUID WITH PARSLEY & PINE KERNELS

Place the sultanas in a small bowl, cover with lukewarm water and set aside for 15 minutes to plump up.

Meanwhile, heat the olive oil in a heavy-based saucepan. Add the parsley and garlic and cook over a low heat, stirring frequently, for 3 minutes. Add the squid and cook, stirring occasionally, for 5 minutes.

Increase the heat to medium, pour in the wine and cook until it has almost completely evaporated. Stir in the passata and season to taste with chilli powder and salt. Lower the heat, cover and simmer gently, stirring occasionally, for 45–50 minutes, until the squid is almost tender.

Drain the sultanas and stir them into the saucepan with the pine kernels. Leave to simmer for a further 10 minutes, then serve immediately, garnished with the reserved chopped parsley.

SERVES 4

85 g/3 oz sultanas

5 tbsp olive oil

6 tbsp chopped fresh flat-leaf parsley, plus extra to garnish

2 garlic cloves, finely chopped

800 g/1 lb 12 oz prepared squid, sliced, or squid rings

125 ml/4 fl oz dry white wine

500 g/1 lb 2 oz passata

pinch of chilli powder

85 g/3 oz pine kernels, finely chopped

salt

SEARED SCALLOPS IN GARLIC BROTH

Combine the garlic cloves, celery, carrot, onion, peppercorns, parsley stems and water in a saucepan with a good pinch of salt. Bring to the boil, reduce the heat and simmer, partially covered, for 30–45 minutes.

Strain the stock into a clean saucepan. Taste and adjust the seasoning, and keep hot.

If using sea scallops, slice in half horizontally to form 2 thinner rounds from each. (If the scallops are very large, slice them into 3 rounds.) Sprinkle with salt and pepper.

Heat the oil in a frying pan over a medium–high heat and cook the scallops on one side for 1–2 minutes, until lightly browned and the flesh becomes opaque.

Divide the scallops between 4 warmed shallow bowls, arranging them browned-side up. Ladle the stock over the scallops, then float a few coriander leaves on top. Serve immediately.

SERVES 4

1 large garlic bulb (about 100 g/ 3½ oz), separated into unpeeled cloves

1 celery stick, chopped

1 carrot, chopped

1 onion, chopped

10 peppercorns

5–6 parsley stems

1.2 litres/2 pints water

225 g/8 oz large sea scallops or queen scallops

1 tbsp oil

salt and pepper

fresh coriander leaves, to garnish

ROASTED
SEAFOOD

Preheat the oven to 200°C/400°F/Gas Mark 6.

Scrub the potatoes to remove any dirt. Cut any large potatoes in half. Parboil the potatoes in a saucepan of boiling water for 10–15 minutes. Place the potatoes in a large roasting tin together with the onions, courgettes, garlic, lemons and rosemary sprigs.

Pour over the oil and toss to coat all the vegetables. Roast in the oven for 30 minutes, turning occasionally, until the potatoes are tender.

Once the potatoes are tender, add the prawns, squid and tomatoes, tossing to coat them in the oil, and roast for 5 minutes. All the vegetables should be cooked through and slightly charred for full flavour. Transfer the roasted seafood and vegetables to warmed serving plates and serve hot.

SERVES 4

600 g/1 lb 5 oz new potatoes

3 red onions, cut into wedges

2 courgettes, cut into chunks

8 garlic cloves, peeled but
   left whole

2 lemons, cut into wedges

4 fresh rosemary sprigs

4 tbsp olive oil

350 g/12 oz unpeeled raw prawns

2 small raw squid, cut into rings

4 tomatoes, quartered

MOROCCAN
FISH TAGINE

FISH & SEAFOOD

Heat the olive oil in a flameproof casserole. Add the onion and cook gently over a very low heat, stirring occasionally, for 10 minutes, or until softened, but not coloured. Add the saffron, cinnamon, ground coriander, cumin and turmeric and cook for a further 30 seconds, stirring constantly.

Add the tomatoes and fish stock and stir well. Bring to the boil, reduce the heat, cover and simmer for 15 minutes. Uncover and simmer for 20–35 minutes, or until thickened.

Cut each red mullet in half, then add the fish pieces to the casserole, pushing them down into the liquid. Simmer the stew for a further 5–6 minutes, or until the fish is just cooked.

Carefully stir in the olives, preserved lemon and chopped coriander. Season to taste with salt and pepper and serve immediately with couscous.

SERVES 4

2 tbsp olive oil

1 large onion, finely chopped

pinch of saffron threads

$\frac{1}{2}$ tsp ground cinnamon

1 tsp ground coriander

$\frac{1}{2}$ tsp ground cumin

$\frac{1}{2}$ tsp ground turmeric

200 g/7 oz canned chopped tomatoes

300 ml/10 fl oz fish stock

4 small red mullet, cleaned, boned and heads and tails removed

55 g/2 oz stoned green olives

1 tbsp chopped preserved lemon

3 tbsp chopped fresh coriander

salt and pepper

freshly cooked couscous, to serve

GOAN-STYLE SEAFOOD CURRY

Heat the oil in a wok or large frying pan over a high heat. Add the mustard seeds and stir them around for about 1 minute, or until they jump. Stir in the curry leaves.

Add the shallots and garlic and stir for about 5 minutes, or until the shallots are golden. Stir in the turmeric, coriander and chilli powder and continue stirring for about 30 seconds.

Add the dissolved creamed coconut. Bring to the boil, then reduce the heat to medium and stir for about 2 minutes.

Reduce the heat to low, add the fish and simmer for 1 minute, spooning the sauce over the fish and very gently stirring it around. Add the prawns and continue to simmer for 4–5 minutes longer until the fish flesh flakes easily and the prawns turn pink and curl.

Add half the lime juice, then taste and add more lime juice and salt to taste. Sprinkle with the lime rind and serve with lime wedges.

SERVES 4–6

3 tbsp vegetable or groundnut oil

1 tbsp black mustard seeds

12 fresh curry leaves or
    1 tbsp dried

6 shallots, finely chopped

1 garlic clove, crushed

1 tsp ground turmeric

½ tsp ground coriander

¼–½ tsp chilli powder

140 g/5 oz creamed coconut,
    grated and dissolved in
    300 ml/10 fl oz boiling water

500 g/1 lb 2 oz skinless, boneless
    white fish, such as monkfish or
    cod, cut into large chunks

450 g/1 lb large raw prawns,
    peeled and deveined

finely grated rind and juice
    of 1 lime

salt

lime wedges, to serve

VEGETABLES

RATATOUILLE

Heat the oil in a large saucepan. Add the onions and cook over a low heat, stirring occasionally, for 5 minutes, or until softened. Add the garlic and cook, stirring frequently for a further 2 minutes.

Add the aubergines, courgettes and peppers. Increase the heat to medium and cook, stirring occasionally, until the peppers begin to colour. Add the bouquet garni, reduce the heat, cover and simmer gently for 40 minutes.

Stir in the chopped tomatoes and season to taste with salt and pepper. Re-cover the saucepan and simmer gently for a further 10 minutes. Remove and discard the bouquet garni. Serve warm or cold.

SERVES 4

150 ml/5 fl oz olive oil

2 onions, sliced

2 garlic cloves, finely chopped

2 medium-sized aubergines, roughly chopped

4 courgettes, roughly chopped

2 yellow peppers, deseeded and chopped

2 red peppers, deseeded and chopped

1 bouquet garni,

3 large tomatoes, peeled, deseeded and roughly chopped

salt and pepper

ROAST SUMMER
VEGETABLES

Preheat the oven to 200°C/400°F/Gas Mark 6. Brush a large ovenproof dish with a little of the oil. Arrange the prepared vegetables in the dish and tuck the garlic cloves and rosemary sprigs among them. Drizzle with the remaining oil and season to taste with plenty of pepper.

Roast the vegetables in the preheated oven for 20–25 minutes, turning once, until they are tender and beginning to turn golden brown.

Serve the vegetables immediately, straight from the dish or transferred to a warmed serving platter, accompanied by crusty bread, if you like, to mop up the juices.

SERVES 4

150 ml/5 fl oz olive oil

1 fennel bulb, cut into wedges

2 red onions, cut into wedges

2 beef tomatoes, cut into wedges

1 aubergine, thickly sliced

2 courgettes, thickly sliced

1 yellow pepper, deseeded and cut into chunks

1 red pepper, deseeded and cut into chunks

1 orange pepper, deseeded and cut into chunks

4 garlic cloves

4 fresh rosemary sprigs

pepper

crusty bread, to serve (optional)

POTATO & MUSHROOM PIE

Preheat the oven to 190°C/375°F/Gas Mark 5. Grease a shallow, round ovenproof dish with the butter.

Layer a quarter of the potatoes in the base of the dish. Arrange one third of the mushrooms on top of the potatoes and sprinkle with one third of the rosemary, chives and garlic. Continue making the layers in the same order, and finish with a layer of potatoes on top.

Pour the double cream evenly over the top of the potatoes. Season to taste with salt and pepper.

Place the dish in the preheated oven, and cook for about 45 minutes, or until the pie is golden brown and piping hot.

Garnish with snipped chives and serve immediately, straight from the dish.

SERVES 4

2 tbsp butter

500 g/1 lb 2 oz waxy potatoes, thinly sliced and parboiled

150 g/5½ oz sliced mixed mushrooms

1 tbsp chopped fresh rosemary, plus extra to garnish

4 tbsp snipped chives, plus extra to garnish

2 garlic cloves, crushed

150 ml/5 fl oz double cream

salt and pepper

AUBERGINE
GRATIN

Heat the oil in a flameproof casserole over a medium heat. Add the onion and cook for 5 minutes, or until soft. Add the garlic and cook for a few seconds, or until just beginning to colour. Using a slotted spoon, transfer the onion mixture to a plate.

Cook the aubergine slices in batches in the same flameproof casserole until they are just lightly browned. Transfer to another plate.

Preheat the oven to 200°C/400°F/Gas Mark 6. Arrange a layer of aubergine slices in the base of the casserole dish or a shallow ovenproof dish. Sprinkle with some of the parsley, thyme, salt and pepper. Add layers of onion, tomatoes and mozzarella, sprinkling parsley, thyme, salt and pepper over each layer.

Continue layering, finishing with a layer of aubergine slices. Sprinkle with the Parmesan. Bake, uncovered, in the preheated oven for 20–30 minutes, or until the top is golden and the aubergines are tender. Serve hot.

SERVES 2

4 tbsp olive oil

2 onions, finely chopped

2 garlic cloves, very finely chopped

2 aubergines, thickly sliced

3 tbsp chopped fresh flat-leaf parsley

½ tsp dried thyme

400 g/14 oz canned chopped tomatoes

175 g/6 oz mozzarella, coarsely grated

6 tbsp freshly grated Parmesan cheese

salt and pepper

PARMESAN RISOTTO WITH MUSHROOMS

Heat the oil in a deep saucepan. Add the rice and cook over a low heat, stirring constantly, for 2–3 minutes, until the grains are thoroughly coated in oil and translucent.

Add the garlic, onion, celery and pepper and cook, stirring frequently, for 5 minutes. Add the mushrooms and cook for 3–4 minutes. Stir in the oregano.

Gradually add the hot stock, a ladle at a time. Stir constantly and add more liquid as the rice absorbs each addition. Increase the heat to medium so that the liquid bubbles. Cook for 20 minutes, or until all the liquid is absorbed and the rice is creamy. Add the sun-dried tomatoes, if using, 5 minutes before the end of the cooking time and season to taste with salt and pepper.

Remove the risotto from the heat and stir in half the Parmesan until it melts. Transfer the risotto to warmed bowls. Top with the remaining cheese, garnish with flat-leaf parsley and serve immediately.

SERVES 6

2 tbsp olive oil or vegetable oil

225 g/8 oz risotto rice

2 garlic cloves, crushed

1 onion, chopped

2 celery sticks, chopped

1 red or green pepper, deseeded and chopped

225 g/8 oz mushrooms, thinly sliced

1 tbsp chopped fresh oregano or 1 tsp dried oregano

1 litre/1¾ pints vegetable stock

55 g /2 oz sun-dried tomatoes in olive oil, drained and chopped (optional)

55 g/2 oz finely grated Parmesan cheese

salt and pepper

fresh flat-leaf parsley sprigs or bay leaves, to garnish

EGG-FRIED RICE WITH VEGETABLES

Heat the oil in a wok or large frying pan and fry the garlic and chillies for 2–3 minutes.

Add the mushrooms, mangetout and baby sweetcorn and stir-fry for 2–3 minutes before adding the soy sauce, sugar and basil. Stir in the rice.

Push the mixture to one side of the wok. Add the eggs to the wok and stir until lightly set before combining with the rice mixture.

If you wish to make the optional crispy onion topping, heat the oil in another frying pan and sauté the onions until crispy and brown. Serve the rice topped with the onions.

142

SERVES 4

2 tbsp vegetable or groundnut oil

2 garlic cloves, finely chopped

2 fresh red chillies, deseeded and chopped

115 g/4 oz mushrooms, sliced

50 g/2 oz mangetout, halved

50 g/2 oz baby sweetcorn, halved

3 tbsp Thai soy sauce

1 tbsp palm sugar or soft, light brown sugar

a few Thai basil leaves

350 g/12 oz rice, cooked and cooled

2 eggs, beaten

crispy onion topping (optional)

2 tbsp vegetable or groundnut oil

2 onions, sliced

SPICED
BASMATI PILAU

Place the rice in a sieve and wash well under cold running water. Drain. Trim off most of the broccoli stalk and cut the head into small florets, then quarter the stalk lengthways and cut diagonally into 1-cm/½-inch pieces.

Heat the oil in a large saucepan. Add the onions and broccoli stalks and cook over a low heat, stirring frequently, for 3 minutes. Add the mushrooms, rice, garlic and spices and cook for 1 minute, stirring, until the rice is coated in oil.

Add the stock and season to taste with salt and pepper. Stir in the broccoli florets and return the mixture to the boil. Cover, reduce the heat and cook over a low heat for 15 minutes without uncovering the pan.

Remove the pan from the heat and leave the pilau to stand for 5 minutes without uncovering. Remove the whole spices, add the raisins and pistachios and gently fork through to fluff up the grains. Serve the pilau hot.

SERVES 4

500 g/1 lb 2 oz basmati rice

175 g/6 oz broccoli, trimmed

6 tbsp vegetable oil

2 large onions, chopped

225 g/8 oz mushrooms, sliced

2 garlic cloves, crushed

6 cardamom pods, split

6 whole cloves

8 black peppercorns

1 cinnamon stick or piece of cassia bark

1 tsp turmeric

1.2 litres/2 pints vegetable stock or water

60 g/2 oz seedless raisins

60 g/2 oz unsalted pistachio nuts, roughly chopped

salt and pepper

MOROCCAN
STEW

Heat the oil in a large, heavy-based saucepan with a tight-fitting
lid and cook the onion, garlic, chilli and aubergine, stirring
frequently, for 5–8 minutes until softened.

Add the cumin, coriander and saffron and cook, stirring
constantly, for 2 minutes. Bruise the cinnamon stick.

Add the cinnamon, squash, sweet potatoes, prunes, 450 ml/
16 fl oz of the stock and the tomatoes to the saucepan and
bring to the boil. Reduce the heat, cover and simmer, stirring
occasionally, for 20 minutes. Add the chickpeas to the saucepan
and cook for a further 10 minutes, adding more stock if
necessary. Discard the cinnamon and serve garnished with the
fresh coriander.

SERVES 4

2 tbsp olive oil

1 Spanish onion, finely chopped

2–4 garlic cloves, crushed

1 fresh red chilli, deseeded
    and sliced

1 aubergine, about 225 g/8 oz, cut
    into small chunks

1 tsp ground cumin

1 tsp ground coriander

pinch of saffron threads

1–2 cinnamon sticks

½–1 butternut squash, about
    450 g/1 lb, peeled, deseeded
    and cut into small chunks

225 g/8 oz sweet potatoes, peeled
    and cut into small chunks

85 g/3 oz ready-to-eat prunes

450–600 ml/16 fl oz–1 pint
    vegetable stock

4 tomatoes, chopped

400 g/14 oz canned chickpeas,
    drained and rinsed

1 tbsp chopped fresh coriander,
    to garnish

POTATO & LEMON CASSEROLE

Heat the olive oil in a flameproof casserole. Add the onions and sauté over a medium heat, stirring frequently, for 3 minutes.

Add the garlic and cook for 30 seconds. Stir in the ground cumin, ground coriander and cayenne and cook, stirring constantly, for 1 minute.

Add the carrot, turnips, courgette and potatoes and stir to coat in the oil.

Add the lemon juice and rind and the stock. Season to taste with salt and pepper. Cover and cook over a medium heat, stirring occasionally, for 20–30 minutes until tender.

Remove the lid, sprinkle in the chopped fresh coriander and stir well. Serve immediately.

SERVES 4

100 ml/3½ fl oz olive oil

2 red onions, cut into 8 wedges

3 garlic cloves, crushed

2 tsp ground cumin

2 tsp ground coriander

pinch of cayenne pepper

1 carrot, thickly sliced

2 small turnips, quartered

1 courgette, sliced

500 g/1 lb 2 oz potatoes, thickly sliced

juice and grated rind of 2 large lemons

300 ml/10 fl oz vegetable stock

2 tbsp chopped fresh coriander

salt and pepper

LENTIL & RICE CASSEROLE

VEGETABLES

Place the lentils, rice and stock in a large flameproof casserole and cook over a low heat, stirring occasionally, for 20 minutes.

Add the leek, garlic, tomatoes and their can juice, ground cumin, chilli powder, garam masala, sliced pepper, broccoli, baby sweetcorn and French beans to the pan.

Bring the mixture to the boil, reduce the heat, cover and simmer for a further 10–15 minutes or until the vegetables are tender.

Add the shredded basil and season to taste with salt and pepper.

Garnish with fresh basil sprigs and serve immediately.

SERVES 4

225 g/8 oz red lentils

55 g/2 oz long-grain rice

1.2 litres/2 pints vegetable stock

1 leek, cut into chunks

3 garlic cloves, crushed

400 g/14 oz canned chopped
   tomatoes

1 tsp ground cumin

1 tsp chilli powder

1 tsp garam masala

1 red pepper, deseeded and sliced

100 g/3½ oz small broccoli florets

8 baby sweetcorn, halved
   lengthways

55 g/2 oz French beans, halved

1 tbsp shredded fresh basil

salt and pepper

fresh basil sprigs, to garnish

VEGETABLE
GOULASH

Put the sun-dried tomatoes in a small heatproof bowl, cover with almost boiling water and leave to soak for 15–20 minutes. Drain, reserving the soaking liquid.

Heat the oil in a large, heavy-based saucepan, with a tight-fitting lid, and cook the chillies, garlic and vegetables, stirring frequently, for 5–8 minutes until softened. Blend the tomato purée with a little of the stock in a jug and pour over the vegetable mixture, then add the remaining stock, lentils, the sun-dried tomatoes and their soaking liquid, and the paprika.

Bring to the boil, then reduce the heat, cover and simmer for 15 minutes. Add the fresh tomatoes and simmer for a further 15 minutes, or until the vegetables and lentils are tender. Serve topped with spoonfuls of soured cream, accompanied by crusty bread.

SERVES 4

15 g/½ oz sun-dried tomatoes, chopped

2 tbsp olive oil

½–1 tsp crushed dried chillies

2–3 garlic cloves, chopped

1 large onion, cut into small wedges

1 small celeriac, cut into small chunks

225 g/8 oz carrots, sliced

225 g/8 oz new potatoes, scrubbed and cut into chunks

1 small acorn squash, deseeded, peeled and cut into small chunks

300 ml/10 fl oz vegetable stock

450 g/1 lb canned Puy or green lentils, drained and rinsed

1–2 tsp hot paprika

2 tbsp tomato purée

450 g/1 lb ripe tomatoes

soured cream, to garnish

crusty bread, to serve

RIBOLLITA

Heat the oil in a large saucepan and cook the onions, carrots and celery for 10–15 minutes, stirring frequently. Add the garlic, thyme, and salt and pepper to taste. Continue to cook for a further 1–2 minutes, until the vegetables are golden and caramelized.

Add the cannellini beans to the pan and pour in the tomatoes. Add enough of the water to cover the vegetables.

Bring to the boil and simmer for 20 minutes. Add the parsley and cavolo nero and cook for a further 5 minutes.

Stir in the bread and add a little more water, if needed. The consistency should be thick.

Taste and adjust the seasoning, if needed. Ladle into warmed serving bowls and serve hot, drizzled with extra virgin olive oil.

SERVES 4

3 tbsp olive oil

2 medium red onions, roughly chopped

3 carrots, sliced

3 celery sticks, roughly chopped

3 garlic cloves, chopped

1 tbsp chopped fresh thyme

400 g/14 oz canned cannellini beans, drained and rinsed

400 g/14 oz canned chopped tomatoes

600 ml/1 pint water or vegetable stock

2 tbsp chopped fresh parsley

500 g/1 lb 2 oz cavolo nero or Savoy cabbage, trimmed and sliced

1 small day-old ciabatta loaf, torn into small pieces

salt and pepper

extra virgin olive oil, to serve

TUSCAN BEAN
STEW

Trim the fennel and reserve any feathery fronds, then cut the bulb into small strips. Heat the oil in a large, heavy-based saucepan with a tight-fitting lid, and cook the onion, garlic, chilli and the fennel strips, stirring frequently, for 5–8 minutes, or until softened.

Add the aubergine and cook, stirring frequently, for 5 minutes. Blend the tomato purée with a little of the stock in a jug and pour over the fennel mixture, then add the remaining stock, and the tomatoes, vinegar and oregano. Bring to the boil, then reduce the heat, cover and simmer for 15 minutes, or until the tomatoes have begun to collapse.

Drain and rinse the beans, then drain again. Add them to the pan with the yellow pepper, courgette and olives. Simmer for a further 15 minutes, or until all the vegetables are tender. Taste and adjust the seasoning. Scatter with the Parmesan cheese shavings and serve garnished with the reserved fennel fronds, accompanied by crusty bread.

SERVES 4

1 large fennel bulb

2 tbsp olive oil

1 red onion, cut into small wedges

2–4 garlic cloves, sliced

1 fresh green chilli, deseeded and chopped

1 small aubergine, about 225 g/ 8 oz, cut into chunks

2 tbsp tomato purée

600 ml/1 pint vegetable stock

450 g/1 lb ripe tomatoes

1 tbsp balsamic vinegar

a few sprigs fresh oregano

400 g/14 oz canned borlotti beans

400 g/14 oz canned flageolet beans

1 yellow pepper, deseeded and cut into small strips

1 courgette, sliced into half moons

55 g/2 oz stoned black olives

25 g/1 oz Parmesan cheese, freshly shaved

salt and pepper

crusty bread, to serve

KIDNEY BEAN, PUMPKIN & TOMATO STEW

158

Pick over the beans, cover generously with cold water and leave to soak for 6 hours or overnight. Drain the beans, put in a saucepan and add enough cold water to cover by 5 cm/2 inches. Bring to the boil and boil for 10 minutes. Drain and rinse well.

Heat the oil in a large saucepan over a medium heat. Add the onions, cover and cook for 3–4 minutes, until they are just softened, stirring occasionally. Add the garlic, celery and carrot, and continue cooking for 2 minutes.

Add the water, drained beans, tomato purée, thyme, oregano, cumin and bay leaf. When the mixture begins to bubble, reduce the heat to low. Cover and simmer gently for 1 hour, stirring occasionally.

Stir in the tomatoes, pumpkin and chilli purée and continue simmering for a further hour, or until the beans and pumpkin are tender, stirring from time to time.

Season to taste with salt and pepper and stir in a little more chilli purée, if liked. Ladle the soup into bowls, garnish with coriander and serve.

SERVES 4–6

250 g/9 oz dried kidney beans

1 tbsp olive oil

2 onions, finely chopped

4 garlic cloves, finely chopped

1 celery stick, thinly sliced

1 carrot, halved and thinly sliced

1.2 litres/2 pints water

2 tsp tomato purée

$\frac{1}{8}$ tsp dried thyme

$\frac{1}{8}$ tsp dried oregano

$\frac{1}{8}$ tsp ground cumin

1 bay leaf

400 g/14 oz canned chopped tomatoes

250 g/9 oz peeled pumpkin flesh, diced

$\frac{1}{4}$ tsp chilli purée, or to taste

salt and pepper

fresh coriander leaves, to garnish

DESSERTS

APPLE & BLACKBERRY CRUMBLE

Preheat the oven to 190°C/375°F/Gas Mark 5.

Peel and core the apples and cut into chunks. Place in a bowl with the blackberries, muscovado sugar and cinnamon and mix together, then transfer to an ovenproof baking dish.

To make the crumble topping, sift the self-raising flour into a bowl and stir in the wholemeal flour. Add the unsalted butter and rub in with your fingers until the mixture resembles fine breadcrumbs. Stir in the demerara sugar.

Spread the crumble over the fruit and bake in the preheated oven for 40–45 minutes, or until the apples are soft and the crumble is golden brown and crisp.

Serve hot with cream.

SERVES 4

900 g/2 lb cooking apples, peeled and sliced

300 g/10½ blackberries, fresh or frozen

55 g/2 oz light muscovado sugar

1 tsp ground cinnamon

single or double cream, to serve

crumble topping

85 g/3 oz self-raising flour

85 g/3 oz plain wholemeal flour

115 g/4 oz unsalted butter

55 g/2 oz demerara sugar

RHUBARB
CRUMBLE

Preheat the oven to 190°C/375°F/Gas Mark 5.

Cut the rhubarb into 2.5-cm/1-inch lengths and place in a 1.7-litre/3-pint ovenproof dish with the sugar and the orange rind and juice.

Make the crumble topping by placing the flour in a mixing bowl and rubbing in the unsalted butter until the mixture resembles breadcrumbs. Stir in the sugar and the ginger.

Spread the crumble evenly over the fruit and press down lightly using a fork. Bake in the centre of the oven on a baking tray for 25–30 minutes until the crumble is golden brown.

Serve warm with cream.

SERVES 6

900 g/2 lb rhubarb

115 g/4 oz caster sugar

grated rind and juice of
  1 orange

cream, yogurt or custard,
  to serve

crumble topping

225 g/8 oz plain or
  wholemeal flour

115 g/4 oz unsalted butter

115 g/4 oz soft brown sugar

1 tsp ground ginger

APRICOT
CRUMBLE

Preheat the oven to 200°C/400°F/Gas Mark 6. Grease a 1.2-litre/ 2-pint ovenproof dish with a little unsalted butter.

Put the unsalted butter and the sugar in a saucepan and melt together, stirring, over a low heat. Add the apricots and cinnamon, cover the saucepan and simmer for 5 minutes.

To make the crumble topping, put the flour in a bowl and rub in the unsalted butter. Stir in the sugar and then the hazelnuts.

Remove the fruit from the heat and arrange in the bottom of the prepared dish. Sprinkle the crumble topping evenly over the fruit until it is covered all over. Transfer to the preheated oven and bake for about 25 minutes until golden.

Serve hot with fresh clotted cream.

SERVES 6

75 g/2½ oz unsalted butter, plus extra for greasing

100 g/3½ oz brown sugar

500 g/1 lb 2 oz fresh apricots, stoned and sliced

1 tsp ground cinnamon

fresh clotted cream, to serve

crumble topping

175 g/6 oz wholemeal flour

50 g/1¾ oz unsalted butter

75 g/2½ oz brown sugar

50 g/1¾ oz hazelnuts, toasted and finely chopped

SHERRIED NECTARINE DESSERT

Preheat the oven to 200°C/400°F/Gas Mark 6.

Using a sharp knife, halve the nectarines, remove and discard the stones, then cut the flesh into fairly thick slices. Put the nectarine slices into an ovenproof pie dish, sprinkle over the sugar and sweet sherry, and cook in the preheated oven for 5–10 minutes until heated through.

To make the crumble topping, put the flour and sugar in a large bowl, then quickly mix in the melted butter until crumbly. Carefully arrange the crumble over the nectarines in an even layer – keep your touch light or the crumble will sink into the filling and go mushy. Scatter a little more sugar over the top, then transfer to the preheated oven and bake for 25–30 minutes, or until the crumble topping is golden brown.

Serve hot with generous spoonfuls of crème fraîche.

SERVES 4

6 nectarines

25 g/1 oz demerara sugar

2 tbsp sweet sherry

crème fraîche, to serve

crumble topping

185 g/6½ oz plain flour

55 g/2 oz demerara sugar, plus extra for sprinkling

100 g/3½ oz unsalted butter, melted

GOOSEBERRY & PISTACHIO NUT DESSERT

Preheat the oven to 200°C/400°F/Gas Mark 6.

Top and tail the gooseberries. Put them in an ovenproof pie dish, pour over the honey and cook in the preheated oven for 5–10 minutes until heated through.

Put the caster sugar, orange juice, orange zest and water in a small saucepan and bring to the boil, stirring, over a medium heat. Reduce the heat and simmer for 5 minutes, then remove from the heat and leave to cool.

Meanwhile, to make the crumble topping, put the flour in a bowl, then use your fingertips to rub in the butter until crumbly. Stir in 4 tablespoons of the demerara sugar and the pistachio nuts.

Pour the cooled orange syrup over the gooseberries, then lightly sprinkle over the crumble mixture in an even layer. Do not press the crumble into the syrup or it will become mushy. Sprinkle over the remaining demerara sugar.

Bake in the preheated oven for 25–30 minutes or until the crumble topping is golden brown. Remove from the oven, decorate with strips of orange rind and serve with créme fraîche.

SERVES 4

400 g/14 oz gooseberries

1 tbsp honey

85 g/3 oz caster sugar

1 tbsp orange juice

1 tbsp grated orange zest

6 tbsp water

thin strips of orange rind, to decorate

créme fraîche, to serve

crumble topping

115 g/4 oz self-raising flour

100 g/3½ oz unsalted butter, diced

5 tbsp demerara sugar

50 g/1¾ oz pistachio nuts, finely chopped

FRUIT COBBLER

Preheat the oven to 200°C/400°F/Gas Mark 6.

Pick over the fruit, mix with the caster sugar and cornflour and put in a 25-cm/10-inch shallow, ovenproof dish.

To make the cobbler topping, sift the flour, baking powder and salt into a large bowl. Rub in the unsalted butter until the mixture resembles breadcrumbs, then stir in the caster sugar. Pour in the buttermilk and mix to a soft dough.

Drop spoonfuls of the dough on top of the fruit roughly, so that it doesn't completely cover the fruit. Sprinkle with the demerara sugar and bake in the preheated oven for 25–30 minutes until the crust is golden and the fruit is tender.

Remove from the oven and leave to stand for a few minutes before serving with cream.

SERVES 6

900 g/2 lb fresh berries and currants, such as blackberries, blueberries, raspberries, redcurrants and blackcurrants

85–115 g/3–4 oz caster sugar

2 tbsp cornflour

single or double cream, to serve

cobbler topping

200 g/7 oz plain flour

2 tsp baking powder

pinch of salt

55 g/2 oz unsalted butter, diced and chilled

2 tbsp caster sugar

175 ml/6 fl oz buttermilk

1 tbsp demerara sugar

STRAWBERRY CREAM COBBLER

Preheat the oven to 200°C/400°F/Gas Mark 6.

Arrange the strawberries evenly in the bottom of an ovenproof dish, then sprinkle over the sugar and cook in the preheated oven for 5–10 minutes until heated through.

Meanwhile, to make the cobbler topping, sift the flour and salt into a large mixing bowl. Rub in the butter until the mixture resembles fine breadcrumbs, then stir in the sugar. Add the beaten egg, then the sultanas and currants, and mix lightly until incorporated. Stir in enough of the milk to make a smooth dough. Transfer to a clean, lightly floured board, knead lightly, then roll out to a thickness of about 1 cm/½ inch. Cut out rounds using a 5-cm/2-inch biscuit cutter. Arrange the dough rounds over the strawberries, then brush the tops with a little milk.

Bake in the preheated oven for 25–30 minutes, or until the cobbler topping has risen and is lightly golden. Serve hot with clotted cream.

SERVES 4

800 g/1 lb 12 oz strawberries, hulled and halved

50 g/1¾ oz caster sugar

clotted cream, to serve

cobbler topping

200 g/7 oz self-raising flour, plus extra for dusting

pinch of salt

3 tbsp butter

2 tbsp caster sugar

1 egg, beaten

25 g/1 oz sultanas

25 g/1 oz currants

about 5 tbsp milk, plus extra for glazing

SPICED MANGO & BLUEBERRY COBBLER

Preheat the oven to 200°C/400°F/Gas Mark 6.

Put the mango slices and blueberries in the bottom of an ovenproof dish, then sprinkle over the nutmeg, lime juice and caster sugar. Cook in the preheated oven for 5–10 minutes until heated through.

To make the cobbler topping, sift the flour, salt and cinnamon into a large mixing bowl. Rub in the unsalted butter until the mixture resembles fine breadcrumbs, then mix in the sugar, and the dried blueberries, if using. Add the beaten egg, then stir in enough of the milk to make a smooth dough. Transfer to a clean, lightly floured board, knead lightly, then roll out to a thickness of about 1 cm/½ inch. Cut out rounds using a 5-cm/2-inch biscuit cutter. Arrange the dough rounds over the fruit, then brush the tops with a little milk.

Bake in the preheated oven for 25–30 minutes, or until the cobbler topping has risen and is lightly golden.

Serve hot with warm custard.

SERVES 4

2 ripe mangoes, stoned and cut into fairly thick slices

250 g/9 oz blueberries

½ tsp nutmeg

1 tbsp lime juice

50 g/1¾ oz caster sugar, or to taste

warm custard, to serve

cobbler topping

200 g/7 oz self-raising flour, plus extra for dusting

pinch of salt

½ tsp cinnamon

3 tbsp unsalted butter

2 tbsp caster sugar

3 tbsp dried blueberries (optional)

1 egg, beaten

about 5 tbsp milk, plus extra for glazing

CHOCOLATE BROWNIES

Preheat the oven to 180°C/350°F/Gas Mark 4. Grease and line a 28 x 18-cm/11 x 7-inch rectangular baking tin.

Put the butter and plain chocolate into a heatproof bowl set over a saucepan of gently simmering water until melted. Remove from the heat. Sift the flour into a large bowl, add the sugar and mix well. Stir the eggs into the chocolate mixture, then beat into the flour mixture. Add the nuts, sultanas and chocolate chips and mix well. Spoon evenly into the prepared tin and level the surface.

Bake in the oven for 30 minutes, or until firm. To check whether the mixture is cooked through, insert a skewer into the centre – it should come out clean. If not, return the tin to the oven for a few minutes. Remove from the oven and leave to cool for 15 minutes. Turn out onto a wire rack to cool completely. To decorate, drizzle the melted white chocolate in fine lines over the top, then cut into squares. Leave to set before serving.

MAKES 15

225 g/8 oz butter, diced, plus extra for greasing

150 g/5½ oz plain chocolate, chopped

225 g/8 oz self-raising flour

125 g/4½ oz dark muscovado sugar

4 eggs, beaten

60 g/2¼ oz blanched hazelnuts, chopped

60 g/2¼ oz sultanas

100 g/3½ oz plain chocolate chips

115 g/4 oz white chocolate, melted, to decorate

UPSIDE-DOWN TOFFEE APPLE BROWNIES

Preheat the oven to 180°C/350°F/Gas Mark 4. Grease a 23-cm/ 9-inch square shallow baking tin.

For the topping, place the muscovado sugar and butter in a small pan and heat gently, stirring, until melted. Pour into the prepared tin. Arrange the apple slices over the mixture.

For the brownies, place the butter and sugar in a bowl and beat well until pale and fluffy. Beat in the eggs gradually.

Sift together the flour, baking powder, bicarbonate of soda and mixed spice, and fold into the mixture. Stir in the apples and nuts.

Pour into the prepared tin and bake for 35–40 minutes, until firm and golden. Cool in the tin for 10 minutes, then turn out and cut into squares.

MAKES 9

toffee apple topping

85 g/3 oz light muscovado sugar

55 g/2 oz unsalted butter

1 dessert apple, cored and
    thinly sliced

brownies

115 g/4 oz unsalted butter,
    plus extra for greasing

175 g/6 oz light muscovado sugar

2 eggs, beaten

200 g/7 oz plain flour

1 tsp baking powder

½ tsp bicarbonate of soda

1½ tsp ground mixed spice

2 eating apples, peeled and
    coarsely grated

85 g/3 oz hazelnuts, chopped

CHOCOLATE MARSHMALLOW FINGERS

Put the digestive biscuits in a polythene bag and, using a rolling pin, crush into small pieces.

Put the chocolate, butter, sugar, cocoa and honey in a saucepan and heat gently until melted. Remove from the heat and leave to cool slightly.

Stir the crushed biscuits into the chocolate mixture until well mixed. Add the marshmallows and mix well, then finally stir in the chocolate chips.

Turn the mixture into a 20-cm/8-inch square baking tin and lightly smooth the top. Put in the refrigerator and leave to chill for 2–3 hours, until set. Cut into fingers before serving.

MAKES 18

350 g/12 oz digestive biscuits

125 g/4½ oz plain chocolate, broken into pieces

225 g/8 oz butter

25 g/1 oz caster sugar

2 tbsp cocoa powder

2 tbsp honey

55 g/2 oz mini marshmallows

100 g/3½ oz white chocolate chips

RICH VANILLA
ICE CREAM

Pour the whipping cream into a large heavy-based saucepan.
Split open the vanilla pod and scrape out the seeds into the
cream, then add the whole vanilla pod, too. Bring almost to the
boil, then remove from the heat and leave to infuse for
30 minutes.

Put the egg yolks and sugar in a large bowl and whisk together
until pale and the mixture leaves a trail when the whisk is lifted.
Remove the vanilla pod from the cream, then slowly add the
cream to the egg mixture, stirring all the time with a wooden
spoon. Strain the mixture into the rinsed-out saucepan or a
double boiler and cook over a low heat for 10–15 minutes, stirring
all the time, until the mixture thickens enough to coat the back
of the spoon. Do not allow the mixture to boil or it will curdle.
Remove the custard from the heat and leave to cool for at least
1 hour, stirring from time to time to prevent a skin from forming.

If using an ice cream machine, churn the cold custard in the
machine following the manufacturer's instructions. Alternatively,
freeze the custard in a freezerproof container, uncovered, for
1–2 hours, or until it begins to set around the edges. Turn
the custard into a bowl and stir with a fork or beat in a food
processor until smooth. Return to the freezer and freeze.

SERVES 4–6

600 ml/1 pint whipping cream or
   300 ml/10 fl oz double cream
   and 300 ml/10 fl oz single cream

1 vanilla pod

4 large egg yolks

115 g/4 oz caster sugar

CHOCOLATE
ICE CREAM

Pour the milk into a large heavy-based saucepan, split open the vanilla pod and scrape out the seeds into the milk and then add the whole vanilla pod, too. Bring almost to the boil then remove from the heat and leave to infuse for 30 minutes. Remove the vanilla pod from the milk. Break the chocolate into the milk and heat gently, stirring all the time, until melted and smooth.

Put the egg yolks and sugar in a large bowl and whisk together until pale and the mixture leaves a trail when the whisk is lifted. Slowly add the chocolate mixture, stirring all the time with a wooden spoon. Strain the mixture into the rinsed-out saucepan or a double boiler and cook over a low heat for 10–15 minutes, stirring all the time, until the mixture thickens enough to coat the back of a wooden spoon. Do not allow the mixture to boil or it will curdle. Remove the custard from the heat and leave to cool for at least 1 hour, stirring from time to time to prevent a skin from forming. Meanwhile, whip the cream until it holds its shape. Keep in the refrigerator until ready to use.

If using an ice cream machine, fold the whipped cream into the cold custard, then churn the mixture in the machine following the manufacturer's instructions. Alternatively, freeze the custard in a freezerproof container, uncovered, for 1–2 hours, or until it begins to set around the edges. Turn the custard into a bowl and stir with a fork or beat in a food processor until smooth. Fold in the whipped cream. Return to the freezer and freeze for a further 2–3 hours, or until firm.

SERVES 4–6

300 ml/10 fl oz milk

1 vanilla pod

100 g/3½ oz plain chocolate

3 egg yolks

85 g/3 oz caster sugar

300 ml/10 fl oz double cream

HONEYCOMB
ICE CREAM

Grease a baking tray. Put the sugar and syrup in a heavy-based saucepan and heat gently until the sugar melts, then boil for 1–2 minutes, or until beginning to caramelize, being careful not to allow the mixture to burn. Stir in the bicarbonate of soda, then immediately pour the mixture onto the prepared baking tray but do not spread. Leave for about 10 minutes until cold.

When the honeycomb is cold, put in a strong polythene bag and crush into small pieces, using a rolling pin or meat mallet. Whip the cream until it holds its shape, then whisk in the condensed milk.

If using an ice cream machine, churn the mixture in the machine following the manufacturer's instructions. Just before the ice cream freezes, add the honeycomb pieces. Alternatively, freeze the mixture in a freezerproof container, uncovered, for 1–2 hours, or until it begins to set around the edges. Turn the mixture into a bowl and stir with a fork or beat in a food processor until smooth. Fold in the honeycomb pieces. Return to the freezer and freeze for a further 2–3 hours, or until firm.

DESSERTS

188

SERVES 6–8

butter, for greasing

85 g/3 oz granulated sugar

2 tbsp golden syrup

1 tsp bicarbonate of soda

400 ml/14 fl oz whipping cream

1 can condensed milk

INDEX

apples
apple & blackberry crumble 162
upside-down toffee apple
brownies 180
apricots
apricot crumble 166
chicken tagine 86
Asian lamb soup 22
aubergines
aubergine gratin 138
chicken tagine 86
Moroccan stew 146
ratatouille 132
roast summer vegetables 134
roasted monkfish 104
Thai green chicken curry 90
Tuscan bean stew 156

bacon
bacon & lentil soup 20
chicken in white wine 74
coq au vin 76
monkfish parcels 102
balti chicken 88
beans
Tuscan bean stew 156
see also borlotti beans; cannellini
beans; kidney beans
beansprouts
Asian lamb soup 22
prawn laksa 112
Thai chicken-coconut soup 28
beef
beef goulash soup 18
beef in beer with herb
dumplings 50
beef stroganoff 44
chilli con carne 46
pepper pot-style stew 48
pot roast with potatoes & dill 42
blackberries
apple & blackberry crumble 162
fruit cobbler 172
blackcurrants: fruit cobbler 172
blueberries
fruit cobbler 172
spiced mango & blueberry
cobbler 176
borlotti beans
minestrone 14
Tuscan bean stew 156
bouillabaisse 36
broccoli
lentil & rice casserole 150
spiced basmati pilau 144

cabbage
chunky vegetable soup 12
minestrone 14
ribollita 154
cannellini beans
Italian turkey cutlets 92
ribollita 154
sausage & bean casserole 56
capers: Mediterranean swordfish 106
carrots
bacon & lentil soup 20
beef goulash soup 18
beef in beer with herb dumplings 50

chunky vegetable soup 12
cock-a-leekie soup 26
duck legs with olives 96
duck with spring onion soup 32
Irish stew 66
kidney bean, pumpkin & tomato
stew 158
lamb shanks 68
pot roast with potatoes & dill 42
potato & lemon casserole 148
ribollita 154
seared scallops in garlic broth 122
turkey & lentil soup 30
vegetable goulash 152
Catalan fish stew 110
cauliflower: turkey & lentil soup 30
celeriac: vegetable goulash 152
celery
bacon & lentil soup 20
chunky vegetable soup 12
duck jambalaya-style stew 98
duck legs with olives 96
kidney bean, pumpkin & tomato
stew 158
lamb shanks 68
Louisiana chicken 84
Mediterranean swordfish 106
minestrone 14
Parmesan risotto with
mushrooms 140
pepper pot-style stew 48
pot roast with potatoes & dill 42
ribollita 154
seared scallops in garlic broth 122
cheese
aubergine gratin 138
chicken risotto with saffron 80
French onion soup 16
Italian-style roast chicken 72
Parmesan risotto with
mushrooms 140
Tuscan bean stew 156
chicken
balti chicken 88
chicken in white wine 74
chicken risotto with saffron 80
chicken tagine 86
cock-a-leekie soup 26
coq au vin 76
cream of chicken soup 24
hunter's chicken 78
Italian-style roast chicken 72
Louisiana chicken 84
pappardelle with chicken porcini 82
prawn & chicken paella 116
Thai chicken-coconut soup 28
Thai green chicken curry 90
chickpeas
chicken tagine 86
lamb stew with chickpeas 64
Moroccan stew 146
chillies
balti chicken 88
chilli con carne 46
duck jambalaya-style stew 98
egg-fried rice with vegetables 142
lamb shanks 68
Louisiana chicken 84
Moroccan stew 146

pappardelle with chicken porcini 82
pepper pot-style stew 48
prawn laksa 112
prawns with coconut rice 114
Sicilian tuna 108
Thai chicken-coconut soup 28
Tuscan bean stew 156
vegetable goulash 152
chocolate
chocolate brownies 178
chocolate ice cream 186
chocolate marshmallow fingers 182
Mexican turkey 94
chorizo
duck jambalaya-style stew 98
lamb stew with chickpeas 64
prawn & chicken paella 116
chunky vegetable soup 12
cinnamon lamb casserole 62
cock-a-leekie soup 26
coconut
Goan-style seafood curry 128
prawn laksa 112
prawns with coconut rice 114
red curry pork with peppers 58
Thai chicken-coconut soup 28
Thai green chicken curry 90
coq au vin 76
courgettes
Italian-style roast chicken 72
monkfish parcels 102
potato & lemon casserole 148
ratatouille 132
roast summer vegetables 134
roasted monkfish 104
roasted seafood 124
turkey & lentil soup 30
Tuscan bean stew 156
cream of chicken soup 24

duck
duck jambalaya-style stew 98
duck legs with olives 96
duck with spring onion soup 32

egg-fried rice with vegetables 142

fennel
roast summer vegetables 134
Sicilian tuna 108
Tuscan bean stew 156
fish & seafood
bouillabaisse 36
Catalan fish stew 110
Goan-style seafood curry 128
Mediterranean swordfish 106
Moroccan fish tagine 126
salmon & leek soup 38
seafood chowder 34
Sicilian tuna 108
see also monkfish; mussels;
prawns; scallops; squid
French onion soup 16
fruit cobbler 172

Goan-style seafood curry 128
gooseberry & pistachio nut
dessert 170

green beans
  lamb with pears 60
  lentil & rice casserole 150
  prawn & chicken paella 116

ham
  duck jambalaya-style stew 98
  minestrone 14
honey
  chocolate marshmallow fingers 182
  gooseberry & pistachio nut
    dessert 170
honeycomb ice cream 188
hunter's chicken 78

ice cream
  chocolate ice cream 186
  honeycomb ice cream 188
  rich vanilla ice cream 184
Irish stew 66
Italian turkey cutlets 92
Italian-style roast chicken 72

kidney beans
  chilli con carne 46
  kidney bean, pumpkin & tomato
    stew 158

lamb
  Asian lamb soup 22
  cinnamon lamb casserole 62
  Irish stew 66
  lamb shanks 68
  lamb stew with chickpeas 64
  lamb with pears 60
leeks
  cock-a-leekie soup 26
  cream of chicken soup 24
  lentil & rice casserole 150
  salmon & leek soup 38
lemons
  Moroccan fish tagine 126
  potato & lemon casserole 148
  roasted seafood 124
  Sicilian tuna 108
lentils
  bacon & lentil soup 20
  lentil & rice casserole 150
  turkey & lentil soup 30
  vegetable goulash 152
limes
  Goan-style seafood curry 128
  lamb shanks 68
  prawn laksa 112
  spiced mango & blueberry
    cobbler 176
  Thai chicken-coconut soup 28
Louisiana chicken 84

mangetout: egg-fried rice with
    vegetables 142
mangoes: spiced mango & blueberry
    cobbler 176
marshmallows: chocolate
    marshmallow fingers 182
Mediterranean swordfish 106
Mexican turkey 94
minestrone 14
monkfish

bouillabaisse 36
  monkfish parcels 102
  roasted monkfish 104
Moroccan fish tagine 126
Moroccan stew 146
moules marinières 118
mushrooms
  beef stroganoff 44
  chicken in white wine 74
  chicken tagine 86
  chunky vegetable soup 12
  coq au vin 76
  duck with spring onion soup 32
  egg-fried rice with vegetables 142
  hunter's chicken 78
  pappardelle with chicken porcini 82
  paprika pork 54
  Parmesan risotto with
    mushrooms 140
  potato & mushroom pie 136
  prawns with coconut rice 114
  red curry pork with peppers 58
  spiced basmati pilau 144
  turkey & lentil soup 30
mussels
  bouillabaisse 36
  Catalan fish stew 110
  moules marinières 118
  prawn & chicken paella 116
  seafood chowder 34

nectarines: sherried nectarine
    dessert 168
noodles
  prawn laksa 112
  Thai chicken-coconut soup 28
nuts
  apricot crumble 166
  Catalan fish stew 110
  chocolate brownies 178
  gooseberry & pistachio nut
    dessert 170
  spiced basmati pilau 144
  upside-down toffee apple
    brownies 180

okra: pepper pot-style stew 48
olives
  duck legs with olives 96
  Mediterranean swordfish 106
  Moroccan fish tagine 126
  Tuscan bean stew 156
onions
  aubergine gratin 138
  bacon & lentil soup 20
  balti chicken 88
  beef goulash soup 18
  beef in beer with herb
    dumplings 50
  bouillabaisse 36
  Catalan fish stew 110
  chicken in white wine 74
  chicken risotto with saffron 80
  chicken tagine 86
  chilli con carne 46
  chunky vegetable soup 12
  cinnamon lamb casserole 62
  cock-a-leekie soup 26
  coq au vin 76

duck jambalaya-style stew 98
duck legs with olives 96
French onion soup 16
hunter's chicken 78
Irish stew 66
Italian turkey cutlets 92
kidney bean, pumpkin & tomato
    stew 158
lamb shanks 68
lamb stew with chickpeas 64
Louisiana chicken 84
Mediterranean swordfish 106
Mexican turkey 94
minestrone 14
Moroccan fish tagine 126
Moroccan stew 146
paprika pork 54
Parmesan risotto with
    mushrooms 140
pepper pot-style stew 48
pork chops with peppers &
    sweetcorn 52
pot roast with potatoes & dill 42
potato & lemon casserole 148
prawn & chicken paella 116
ratatouille 132
red curry pork with peppers 58
ribollita 154
roast summer vegetables 134
roasted monkfish 104
roasted seafood 124
salmon & leek soup 38
sausage & bean casserole 56
seafood chowder 34
seared scallops in garlic broth 122
Sicilian tuna 108
spiced basmati pilau 144
turkey & lentil soup 30
Tuscan bean stew 156
vegetable goulash 152
see also shallots; spring onions
oranges
  gooseberry & pistachio nut
    dessert 170
  rhubarb crumble 164

pappardelle with chicken porcini 82
paprika pork 54
Parmesan risotto with
    mushrooms 140
pasta
  beef goulash soup 18
  minestrone 14
  pappardelle with chicken porcini 82
pears: lamb with pears 60
peas
  minestrone 14
  prawn & chicken paella 116
pepper pot-style stew 48
peppers
  beef goulash soup 18
  Catalan fish stew 110
  chicken tagine 86
  duck jambalaya-style stew 98
  duck with spring onion soup 32
  Italian turkey cutlets 92
  Italian-style roast chicken 72
  lentil & rice casserole 150
  Louisiana chicken 84

Mexican turkey 94
minestrone 14
monkfish parcels 102
Parmesan risotto with
    mushrooms 140
pepper pot-style stew 48
pork chops with peppers &
    sweetcorn 52
prawn & chicken paella 116
ratatouille 132
red curry pork with peppers 58
roast summer vegetables 134
roasted monkfish 104
sausage & bean casserole 56
turkey & lentil soup 30
Tuscan bean stew 156
pine kernels: squid with parsley &
    pine kernels 120
pork
    paprika pork 54
    pork chops with peppers &
        sweetcorn 52
    red curry pork with peppers 58
pot roast with potatoes & dill 42
potatoes
    bacon & lentil soup 20
    chunky vegetable soup 12
    Irish stew 66
    Italian-style roast chicken 72
    lamb with pears 60
    pot roast with potatoes & dill 42
    potato & lemon casserole 148
    potato & mushroom pie 136
    roasted seafood 124
    salmon & leek soup 38
    vegetable goulash 152
prawns
    bouillabaisse 36
    Catalan fish stew 110
    Goan-style seafood curry 128
    prawn & chicken paella 116
    prawn laksa 112
    prawns with coconut rice 114
    roasted seafood 124
    seafood chowder 34
prunes
    cock-a-leekie soup 26
    Moroccan stew 146
pumpkin
    kidney bean, pumpkin & tomato
        stew 158
    see also squash

raisins & sultanas
    chocolate brownies 178
    cinnamon lamb casserole 62
    Mexican turkey 94
    spiced basmati pilau 144
    squid with parsley & pine
        kernels 120
    strawberry cream cobbler 174
raspberries: fruit cobbler 172
ratatouille 132
red curry pork with peppers 58
redcurrants: fruit cobbler 172
rhubarb crumble 164
ribollita 154
rice

chicken risotto with saffron 80
egg-fried rice with vegetables 142
lentil & rice casserole 150
Parmesan risotto with
    mushrooms 140
prawn & chicken paella 116
prawns with coconut rice 114
spiced basmati pilau 144
rich vanilla ice cream 184
roast summer vegetables 134
roasted monkfish 104
roasted seafood 124

salmon & leek soup 38
sausages
    sausage & bean casserole 56
    see also chorizo
scallops
    bouillabaisse 36
    seared scallops in garlic broth 122
seafood chowder 34
seared scallops in garlic broth 122
shallots
    beef stroganoff 44
    cream of chicken soup 24
    Goan-style seafood curry 128
    moules marinières 118
sherried nectarine dessert 168
Sicilian tuna 108
soups
    Asian lamb soup 22
    bacon & lentil soup 20
    beef goulash soup 18
    bouillabaisse 36
    chunky vegetable soup 12
    cock-a-leekie soup 26
    cream of chicken soup 24
    duck with spring onion soup 32
    French onion soup 16
    minestrone 14
    salmon & leek soup 38
    seafood chowder 34
    Thai chicken-coconut soup 28
    turkey & lentil soup 30
spiced basmati pilau 144
spiced mango & blueberry
    cobbler 176
spring onions
    Asian lamb soup 22
    duck with spring onion soup 32
    prawns with coconut rice 114
    Thai chicken-coconut soup 28
squash
    Moroccan stew 146
    pepper pot-style stew 48
    vegetable goulash 152
    see also pumpkin
squid
    roasted seafood 124
    squid with parsley & pine
        kernels 120
strawberry cream cobbler 174
sweet potatoes: Moroccan stew 146
sweetcorn

chunky vegetable soup 12
egg-fried rice with vegetables 142
lentil & rice casserole 150
pork chops with peppers &
    sweetcorn 52

Thai chicken-coconut soup 28
Thai green chicken curry 90
tomatoes
    Asian lamb soup 22
    aubergine gratin 138
    balti chicken 88
    beef goulash soup 18
    bouillabaisse 36
    Catalan fish stew 110
    chilli con carne 46
    chunky vegetable soup 12
    cinnamon lamb casserole 62
    duck jambalaya-style stew 98
    duck legs with olives 96
    hunter's chicken 78
    Italian turkey cutlets 92
    kidney bean, pumpkin & tomato
        stew 158
    lamb stew with chickpeas 64
    lentil & rice casserole 150
    Louisiana chicken 84
    Mediterranean swordfish 106
    Mexican turkey 94
    minestrone 14
    Moroccan fish tagine 126
    Moroccan stew 146
    pappardelle with chicken porcini 82
    Parmesan risotto with
        mushrooms 140
    pepper pot-style stew 48
    ratatouille 132
    red curry pork with peppers 58
    ribollita 154
    roast summer vegetables 134
    roasted seafood 124
    sausage & bean casserole 56
    squid with parsley & pine
        kernels 120
    turkey & lentil soup 30
    Tuscan bean stew 156
    vegetable goulash 152
turkey
    Italian turkey cutlets 92
    Mexican turkey 94
    turkey & lentil soup 30
turnips
    bacon & lentil soup 20
    potato & lemon casserole 148
Tuscan bean stew 156

upside-down toffee apple
    brownies 180

vegetable goulash 152

yogurt
    balti chicken 88
    cinnamon lamb casserole 62